Genshin

The 100th Year of
Joshu Sasaki Roshi

 *This emblem is an insignia for Kyozan Joshu Sasaki Roshi. The five petals signify an apricot blossom (Kyozan, Roshi's osho name, means "apricot mountain"). The four squares in the center are an emblem of the Sasaki family. The golden border and red centers signify the richness and radiance of the Buddhist teachings.*

Copyright © 2007 Rinzai-ji Incorporated

Printed in USA by Cayuga Press of Ithaca

Design and production paper*Moon* Design

CONTENTS

Introduction	1
I Have No Biography	3
Roshi's Zen Lineage	10
Introduction to the Interview	15
Roshi's Zen Teachings – Interview	20
Walking the 100th Year	33
Rinzai-ji Oshos	43
Rinzai-ji Temples and Centers	49
Some Reflections	61
Anecdotes	79
In Praise of Joshu Roshi's Great Work	85
Letter from the President of Rinzai-ji	87

The 100th Year of Joshu Sasaki Roshi

If you do have that kind of passion to practice, a passion which leads you to clench your teeth in making efforts to clarify this principle, then I also, with strong will, plan to continue the practices of teisho and sanzen with all of you until I die.

THIS ALBUM HAS BEEN PUBLISHED TO COMMEMORATE THE ONE HUNDREDTH BIRTHDAY OF JOSHU SASAKI ROSHI AND THE FORTY-FIFTH YEAR OF HIS TEACHING ZEN IN AMERICA.

LEFT

MIURA JOTEN ROSHI —
THE 23RD KANCHO OF
MYOSHIN-JI AND
JOSHU ROSHI'S TEACHER
1871–1958

RIGHT

BANRYŌ ZENSO —
TEACHER OF JOTEN MIURA
AND GRAND TEACHER OF
JOSHU ROSHI
1848–1935

VI

The 100th Year of Joshu Sasaki Roshi

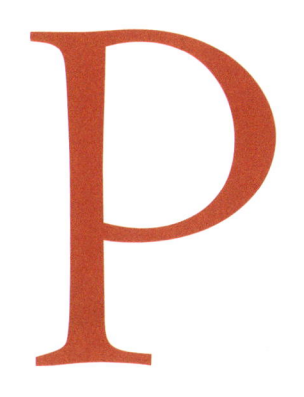

PIERCED BY THE SHADOW OF PAST TEACHERS, SELF DISSOLVING IS ALL I KNOW.
NOW AWAKENED FROM THIS DISSOLUTION, OH WHERE IS MY TRUE TEACHER?
COMINGS AND COMINGS, GOINGS AND GOINGS, MOVING ONLY WITH PERFECT SILENCE.
BUT EVEN SO, I MYSELF HAVE YET TO ARRIVE INTO SILENCE. OH WHAT CAN I DO?

JOSHU ROSHI, MARCH 6, 2007

INTERPRETATION BY ROSHI

MY DIRECT TEACHER IS JOTEN SOKO. JOTEN'S TEACHER IS BANRYŌ ZENSO. NOW, AS I MEET THIS PHOTOGRAPH OF BANRYŌ, A DEEP CRY OF ADMIRATION AND REGRET OVERWHELMS EVERYTHING.

YET AS I AWAKE FROM THIS DREAM OF OVERWHELMING FEELING MIXED WITH ADMIRATION AND REGRET, I YEARN FOR MY TRUE TEACHER. AND SEEKING ALL THROUGH HEAVEN AND EARTH, SILENCE IS ALL I FIND. WAKING AGAIN FROM THIS DREAM, KEENLY KNOWING I MYSELF HAVE YET TO ARRIVE INTO TRUE SILENCE, MY SELF-REPROACH FOR IMPERFECT PRACTICE FILLS EVERYTHING.

FURTHER COMMENT BY ROSHI

WHEN ASKED TO SPEAK OF THIS SORT OF THING I AM FILLED WITH TEARS AND DON'T WANT TO TALK. PEOPLE UNKNOWINGLY EXPRESS THEIR DESIRE TO ASK AND HEAR MY STORY, WITHOUT THOUGHT FOR WHY I WOULDN'T WANT TO SAY IT. I, ON THE OTHER HAND, WOULDN'T ASK ABOUT ANOTHER'S LOVE STORY. EVERYONE WANTS TO HEAR EACH OTHER'S LOVE STORIES, BUT REALLY, THEY ARE NOT FOR SPEAKING. IT IS TOO BITTERLY HEARTBREAKING. LOVE STORIES ARE THE SADDEST. THIS IS WHAT THE POEM IS ABOUT. A LOVE STORY APPEARS IN THIS POEM. THAT IS ENOUGH TO SAY. LOVE STORIES MUST BE SILENT.

The 100th Year of Joshu Sasaki Roshi

Introduction

Forty-five years ago a small Japanese man, a bearer of the Zen wisdom insight, arrived in the United States having made the vow not to die until he had transplanted his viewpoint, the wisdom itself, into this country. Today, the beneficiaries of this man and this vow gather to celebrate the one hundredth year of his visit to the human world. This album is an expression of gratitude by his community, his sangha, to its teacher, the one who has revealed the Buddhist treasures.

The debt of gratitude that one owes to one's spiritual teacher is immeasurable and can never be repaid. This is because, when the deeper dimension of being is opened, there is no gesture in the human world that can reciprocate for that opening. Nevertheless, we bow to Joshu Sasaki Roshi, who, even at the age of one hundred, drags himself to the teaching platform and invites those who have ears to hear, those who have eyes to see and those who have minds to know.

The editor would like to thank the following for their contributions: Arai Fusae for her untiring work of translation, Kogetsu Radin for her patience and insight while editing, Joshi Radin for her wonderful photographs of Roshi and Rinzai-ji members, Josh Swiller for composing Roshi's biography, Glenn Burney for his advice and humor, Kushin Michele Sevik for her organizing and editing the osho material, Parham Arjad-Yeshareem for his eagle eyes, David Shalloway and Kelly Morris for proofreading, Giko Rubin for translating Roshi's poem and commentary, Leslie Carrère and Anne Kilgore for design and production, the Osho Council and the many oshos and Rinzai-ji members who contributed articles and photographs, and the Rinzai-ji Board of Directors for its support of the project.

I HAVE No BIOGRAPHY

Writing a biography of Roshi, writing of the events of his corporal body in this physical world, is like writing about the floor tiles at the Sistine Chapel, like admiring the frame of the Mona Lisa. His life has been devoted to teaching the essence of Zen. The events of his life are simply the packaging in which these teachings have been made available.

"I have no biography," he says when you sit down to question him.

Joshu Roshi was born one hundred years ago into a farming family near Sendai in Miyage Prefecture. When Joshu was thirteen, a brother three years older, the one closest to him in age, passed away. Roshi was close to this brother, and though eighty-seven years have gone by, he still thinks of him.

The death had a profound impact on young Joshu. It stirred up difficult questions: how could God take away someone so strong, so good? Was there really a God? "I really thought that my brother was God," Joshu says. "My brother passed away so I could no longer believe in God."

Roshi once reflected on his early memories. "My mother, where will she go when she passes away, many times I thought.... This father, when he has to pass away, where will he go, many things I wondered...."

At this time, Joshu attended a regular public school. He was late for school each morning because of his chores which included cooking and cleaning for his entire family. His grades were poor. Only in music or singing and mathematics did Joshu receive good grades. This will come as no surprise to the

FARM HOUSE WHERE ROSHI WAS BORN AND RAISED.

The 100th Year of Joshu Sasaki Roshi

DARUMA (BODHIDHARMA)
BY MIURA JOTEN ROSHI,
JOSHU ROSHI'S MASTER

The clouds of delusion dissipate, and even the darkest cave is illuminated.

students who have heard his gorgeous, sonorous chanting and have experienced his fondness for explaining the dharma with the numbers zero, one and two, and the terms plus and minus. ("What is one plus one?" Roshi once asked a monk who was a math professor. "Two," the monk replied. "Zero," answered Roshi.)

Joshu was told upon the death of his brother that "He went to heaven." He could not accept this answer. At the tender age of fourteen, Joshu left public school and entered the Zuiryo-ji monastery.

Zuiryo-ji was five hundred miles away from Sendai in Sapporo in Hokkaido, northern Japan. The master at Zuiryo-ji was Joten Soko Miura Roshi, who later became head of Myoshin-ji, the pre-eminent Rinzai temple complex in Japan.

The young novice was interrogated by the abbot shortly after his arrival. "How old is the Buddha?" asked Joten Soko.

Whether his insight was already deep, or whether he had an extraordinary amount of chutzpa, Joshu replied, "Buddha's age and my age are the same."

The master replied, "This one is ready to start zazen practice."

Roshi tells another story from those first months as a monk. One day, he was cleaning inside a temple building and it started to snow. Snow is common in Sapporo, one of Japan's northernmost cities. That day, Joshu looked out the window at the snow falling, landing on the window glass, melting and disappearing. Where, he wondered, did the snow come from, where did it go? Not in a scientific sense (i.e., heat breaking the bond between water molecules and so forth), but in an experiential sense, Roshi wondered: these snowflakes I see, these family members I loved and lost, where did they originate, where did they go?

Joshu Roshi was ordained an *osho* (priest) at twenty-one, receiving the name of Kyozan, and then practiced as an osho for twenty years at Myoshin-ji in Kyoto. In 1947, at the age of forty, he received authority as a Roshi. In 1953, he became the abbot of Shojo-an in Liyama, an abandoned temple that had fallen into disrepair.

Shojo-an had once been the temple of Hakuin's master, Dokyo Etan. Hakuin is perhaps the most well-known and beloved teacher of the Rinzai school of Zen. Rinzai was a declining tradition when Hakuin began to teach in the early 18th century; he reinvigorated it by strongly focusing on zazen and koan practice. This is an approach that Roshi has continued and he is one of the remaining masters of the form.

Stories are passed down by Joshu Roshi's students of what he was like as a young Roshi in Japan; of the severity and discipline of his instruction, of how young monks under his care would soil themselves in fear when he walked past.

Roshi spent ten years at Shojo-an.

4

The 100th Year of Joshu Sasaki Roshi

In early 1962, two Zen students in Southern California, Gladys Weisbart and Dr. Robert Harmon, contacted Myoshin-ji for a Zen teacher. Roshi was selected by the temple and he arrived at Los Angeles International Airport on July 21, 1962. Roshi was 55 and had never been outside of Japan. He knew only a rudimentary amount of English and carried with him two dictionaries in his sleeves: in his right, a Japanese-to-English edition; in the left, English-to-Japanese.

Roshi went to live in the garage of Dr. Harmon. By day, the garage transformed into a zendo, for which Roshi served as Jikijitsu, Shoji, Tenzo and Densu; at night, it was his home. Over the next six years, a community of students grew around Roshi. Space was often hard to come by and the zendo was moved several times, but more and more students came to practice. In 1967, Roshi conducted his first seven day Dai-sesshin.

In 1968, the building that now houses Rinzai-ji Zen Center was purchased. The building was so rundown that the city of Los Angeles had actually condemned it. With much work, Roshi's students refurbished it and on April 21st of that year, Roshi's sixty-first birthday, it was opened as Cimarron Zen Center.

The center grew rapidly: other nearby buildings were purchased to house students and guests, and then, in 1970, Shozan Marc Joslyn, one of Roshi's students from Claremont and currently an osho, happened upon an old boy scout camp

I Have No Biography

ROSHI WITH JIMMY YAMAMOTO WHO TRANSLATED FOR ROSHI DURING HIS FIRST 10 YEARS IN AMERICA. WHEN THEY MET AGAIN IN 2001, MR. YAMAMOTO — THEN 88 — REMARKED, "I AM ENJOYING THE LAST FEW YEARS OF MY LIFE. OLD AGE DOES NOT LAST VERY LONG. I AM VERY THANKFUL TO ROSHI FOR TEACHING ME ABOUT HUMAN WISDOM AND SHOWING ME MY DESTINY."

in the San Gabriel Mountains east of Los Angeles. The first Dai-sesshin was held at that site in 1970, and the following spring it was formally founded as Mount Baldy Zen Center.

Teaching American students who live in a culture that values individual achievement above all and who must navigate lives replete with financial, familial and psychological pressures has been a constant learning process says Roshi. It is not the world he knew in Japan. He has adapted his teachings to it. If you are married, he teaches, that is truth. If you have a child, that is truth. Don't reject the life you have as some impediment, but recognize it as the manifestation of truth.

In the forty-five years Roshi has lived in America he has taught thousands of students. He oversees several centers, a few of which are situated in some of the country's most stark, beautiful landscapes. None of this Roshi expected when he arrived at the Los Angeles airport with dictionaries in his sleeves. In an interview, he said: "I had the thought to have five or six students who really lived the life of Zen and that would be it. I had no plans to create temples or centers."

Today, Roshi still leads training at three main centers: Rinzai-ji, Mount Baldy, and Bodhi Manda Zen Center in Jemez Springs, New Mexico. Each center has its own personality, folklore and challenges. Rinzai-ji, for example, is located in what is now a peaceful neighborhood, but Dai-sesshins there used to be punctuated by the sound of gunfire.

Recalls one monk of his first Dai-sesshin at Rinzai-ji: "We were awakened by the bell at 3:00 AM. Outside a helicopter was circling the neighborhood with a loudspeaker blasting, 'Come out of the building with your hands raised over your head! Come out of the building with your hands raised over your head!' I thought 'Whew! This is a really strong Shoji here!'"

At Mt. Baldy, the challenges are often environmental: monks and residents have had to evacuate several times in the last decade because of forest fires, and during winter storms, snow can fall at a rate of almost a foot an hour. And Roshi's quarters there didn't even have indoor plumbing for fourteen years!

The formation of Bodhi Manda reveals the impish good-humor which is so much a part of Roshi's being. In the early seventies, a student named Michelle Martin asked him to conduct a dai-sesshin in New Mexico, to which Roshi replied; "You find hot springs, I come." Martin found an old Catholic monastery with a spring for sale and Roshi, true to his word, came and has been coming ever since.

Over the years Roshi has conducted sanzen with and given teisho to students in Canada, Poland, Norway, Austria, Germany, Spain, Belgium, Puerto Rico and New Zealand. He has led sesshins in one hundred-degree heat, in tropical rainstorms, in six-foot snows. He has led sesshins while fighting pneumonia and bronchitis, led a sesshin one week after having his gall bladder removed, another one week after surgery to place a stent in his heart. He has been taken away to emergency rooms in great pain in the night, only to return for the first sanzen in the morning.

These days, Roshi has fewer new students than he did back in the sixties and seventies when the Vietnam War was at its peak and students arrived questioning the very fabric of the society. That doesn't seem as common, Roshi observes, despite the fact that the world continues to manifest pain. Yet he continues. At the age of 100, Roshi still teaches a full schedule, with at least

ROSHI WITH LONG-TIME FRIENDS AND SUPPORTERS (FROM LEFT) DAN SUNADA, DR. MACY, AND DR. HARMON, WHO INVITED ROSHI TO THE UNITED STATES IN 1962.

I Have No Biography

RIGHT

JOSHU ROSHI (FRONT ROW, SECOND FROM RIGHT) PRIOR TO DEPARTURE FOR LOS ANGELES IN 1962

one Dai-sesshin a month, and usually two, each with a teisho and four sanzens a day, and usually with over forty students in attendance.

Age has taken away some things. The fearsome temper of the young Roshi has mellowed. The century-old knees have long ago outgrown the full-lotus seats of youth. Grudgingly, Roshi has had to cut his intake of sake and up his daily vitamins. He cannot walk too far anymore. For years now at Mt. Baldy he has been driven the few hundred yards from his living quarters to the sutra hall. Once inside the sutra hall, he usually relies on the vice abbot to perform the full bows before teisho. But still he teaches. Still he takes up the human form bearing love. Still he prods and chuckles and growls and rings the bell. Where does he get the energy?

He answers: "It is the energy of the absolute and that is the activity of love."

But isn't Roshi pushing too hard? Will he stop? How will he stop? Is there any plan to ease up?

"No," he answers. "If you have that kind of passion to practice, a passion which leads you to clench your teeth in making efforts to clarify this principle, then I also, with strong will, plan to continue the practices of teisho and sanzen with all of you until I die."

He seeks no thanks for doing this practice, which brings us back to the great difficulties of writing a biography on the occasion of Roshi's 100th birthday. You want to praise the man, the vehicle that allows all this to flow forth, but Roshi insists there is no need for praise. You want to hear more about his story, but he says there is no story. He says, "If you want a biography, interview Bush or Clinton." And if you say, "But Roshi, what did you think as a young monk?" he'll whack his stick against the chair and ask you where the Buddha is in that sound.

There, he would say, you will find my true biography.

Then he would ring the bell.

I Have No Biography

Roshi's Zen Lineage

RIGHT

RINZAI-JI

COURTYARD

1. Mahakasyapa
2. Ananda
3. Sanavasa
4. Upagupta
5. Dhritika
6. Micchaka
7. Vasumitra
8. Buddhanandi
9. Buddhamitra
10. Bhikshu Parsva
11. Punyayasas
12. Asvaghosha
13. Bhikshu Kapimala
14. Nagarjuna
15. Kanadeva
16. Arya Rahulata
17. Samghanandi
18. Samghayasas
19. Kumaralata
20. Jayata
21. Vasubandhu

22. Manura
23. Haklanayasas
24. Bhikshu Simha
25. Vasasita
26. Punyamitra
27. Prajnatara
28. Bodhidharma
29. Eka Daiso
30. Sosan Kanshi
31. Doshin Dai-i
32. Gunin Daitan
33. Eno Taikan
34. Nangaku Ejo
35. Baso Doitsu
36. Hyakujo Ekai
37. Obaku Kiun
38. Rinzai Gigen
39. Koke Sonaho
40. Nanin Ekyo
41. Fuketsu Ensho
42. Shuzan Shonen

43. Funyo Zensho
44. Jimyo Soen
45. Yogi Hoe
46. Hakuun Shutan
47. Goso Hoen
48. Tennei Kokugon
49. Kukyu Shoryu
50. Ninnan Donge
51. Mittan Kanketsu
52. Shogan Sogaku
53. Unnan Fugan
54. Kido Chigu
55. Nanpo Shomyo
56. Shuho Myocho
57. Kanzan Egen
58. Jue Sohitsu
59. Muin Soin
60. Nippo Soshun
61. Giten Gensho
62. Sekko Soshin
63. Toyo Eicho

The 100th Year of Joshu Sasaki Roshi

I Have No Biography

Roshi's Zen Lineage

RIGHT

RINZAI-JI

COURTYARD

1. Mahakasyapa
2. Ananda
3. Sanavasa
4. Upagupta
5. Dhritika
6. Micchaka
7. Vasumitra
8. Buddhanandi
9. Buddhamitra
10. Bhikshu Parsva
11. Punyayasas
12. Asvaghosha
13. Bhikshu Kapimala
14. Nagarjuna
15. Kanadeva
16. Arya Rahulata
17. Samghanandi
18. Samghayasas
19. Kumaralata
20. Jayata
21. Vasubandhu

22. Manura
23. Haklanayasas
24. Bhikshu Simha
25. Vasasita
26. Punyamitra
27. Prajnatara
28. Bodhidharma
29. Eka Daiso
30. Sosan Kanshi
31. Doshin Dai-i
32. Gunin Daitan
33. Eno Taikan
34. Nangaku Ejo
35. Baso Doitsu
36. Hyakujo Ekai
37. Obaku Kiun
38. Rinzai Gigen
39. Koke Sonaho
40. Nanin Ekyo
41. Fuketsu Ensho
42. Shuzan Shonen

43. Funyo Zensho
44. Jimyo Soen
45. Yogi Hoe
46. Hakuun Shutan
47. Goso Hoen
48. Tennei Kokugon
49. Kukyu Shoryu
50. Ninnan Donge
51. Mittan Kanketsu
52. Shogan Sogaku
53. Unnan Fugan
54. Kido Chigu
55. Nanpo Shomyo
56. Shuho Myocho
57. Kanzan Egen
58. Jue Sohitsu
59. Muin Soin
60. Nippo Soshun
61. Giten Gensho
62. Sekko Soshin
63. Toyo Eicho

The 100th Year of Joshu Sasaki Roshi

64. Taiga Senkyo
65. Koho Genkun
66. Sensho Zuisho
67. Ian Chisatsu
68. Tozen Soshin
69. Yozan Keiyo
70. Gudo Toshoku
71. Shido Bunan
72. Dokyo Etan
73. Hakuin Ekaku
74. Gasan Jitaku
75. Inzan Ian
76. Taigen Shigen
77. Daisetsu Joen
78. Dokuon Joshu
79. Banryo Zenso
80. Joten Soko
81. Kyozan Joshu

The Zen Lineage

There is really nothing at all difficult about Zen. Just listen carefully to teisho, do zazen and review teisho and you will come to the realization — YES! THIS IS EXACTLY THE WAY IT IS!

When I make this sound — if you are on top of it, at once you will be able to know that this sound is the voice of God, the voice of Buddha. Your zazen practice is to penetrate this sound and know this to be true. When you hear this sound or when you see a flower, you are seeing and hearing together with God, together with Buddha.

The 100th Year of Joshu Sasaki Roshi

The 100th Year of Joshu Sasaki Roshi

AN INTERVIEW WITH Joshu Roshi

INTRODUCTION

This album is a tribute to the life of Joshu Roshi and his ceaseless devotion to teaching the Dharma, the nature of reality. The intention was to present his biography, including pictures and stories, with expressions of gratitude by those who have gathered around to bask in the light of his teachings and presence. But Roshi remarked that if this album were truly to be a gesture to him, it must include what his life is really about – the Dharma teaching itself.

Roshi was asked if he would consent to an interview, a dialogue about his perspective, so that the format would be more casual, and in a certain way, perhaps more accessible, than a teisho, his formal lectures during training periods. He agreed. In early December 2006, we spoke with Roshi for six hours over the course of two days. Fusae Arai served as translator.

Shortly after the interview, Roshi began leading the winter training period at Mount Baldy Zen Center. Attempts were made to verify the accuracy of the translation by reading it back to him. Because of the busy seichu schedule, however, there was not time to do so for the interview or the summary in this introduction. Although the tape of the interview was checked, there may still be mistakes for which we apologize. Had we waited until the end of winter seichu for Roshi to be free again, the album would have been held up well past the celebration of his 100th birthday.

Roshi often expresses his teachings in terms and metaphors which, while familiar to students who have sat and listened to his teisho for many years, may be confusing to others. These longtime practitioners also have had the benefit of zazen and sanzen to help clarify Roshi's teachings and his perspective. Because this album may find its way to readers not familiar with his descriptive style, this explanatory introduction is offered.

Buddhism is the religion of awakening and the teachings about the path to awakening. Roshi points out that the awakening is the self awakening from identifying itself with an activity of mind and seeing its true nature directly.

When the wisdom that knows the Dharma activity is manifest then, for the first time, true mercy is manifest.

In his teachings Roshi continuously drives home the point that the individual self people take themselves to be – the "I am" self – is not fixated; it has no unchanging essence; it is not a "true" self. It is an incomplete self that arises conditionally. What are these conditions? That subject and object are originally unified, that the self and the cosmos are originally one, and that this union is the foundation of everything that appears – all individual selves arise out of a foundation of union with the objective appearances. So if one relates to life from the point of view that the self is an independently existing subject completely separate from the world, this thinking is erroneous and one's whole approach to life based on this view will be problematic and unsatisfying.

Roshi interchangeably uses several metaphors, each conveying a slightly nuanced meaning, to describe the components of this original union: a male activity and a female activity, a plus activity and a minus activity, a subjective activity and an objective activity, and a husband activity and a wife activity. He teaches that what obscures the great vision of the original union of these opposing activities is the unquestioning acceptance of the subjective self as an independent being, rather than recognizing it as an activity of mind which is an interpretation of experience that has not been meditatively examined. To help clarify this mistaken notion Roshi encourages us to contemplate our experience and gain clear insight.

Another term that Roshi uses frequently in his teaching is "activity." Since there are no fixated existences, no real independent selves, Roshi designates events as activities, such as, the activity of being directly connected to God, the activity of living and dying, the activity of emptiness, the activity of mind, the activity of being born. . . . This style of expression emphasizes the utter fluidity of experience and points to the no-self nature of all apparent entities.

When a student begins training, he/she may never have heard these teachings of no-self. While striking his ceremonial fan on the lectern, Roshi invites the student to inquire into this principle by asking, "Where are you when you hear this sound?" What the student has always assumed – I am over here and the sound is over there – is now brought into question. As the student's practice matures, he/she begins to grasp that the world that is appearing as object is inextricably bound to the perceiving subject, and that the self is neither or both.

Subjects experience objects through the five senses and the mind. In each instance, what Roshi calls the "I am self" is a mental interpretation of the experience that locates the self as that which is seeing from behind the eye or hearing from within the ear. However, if one were to analyze sensation, one would not be able to locate the self in that way. What is in back of the eye is a retina which becomes the image of the object – there is no entity. Similarly with hearing and all the other senses, the sense organ always takes the form of the object – the sense object and sense organ are unified. Serene, clear introspection reveals the absence of an independent self in sensation.

One might similarly reflect on the nature of dreams, which Roshi talks about in the interview, wherein the mind projects an originally unified universe (the dream) and then an "I am self" takes up residence as a particular subject within that dream, ignoring the obvious fact that the dream objects appearing as external to that subject are originally one with it.

Roshi teaches that, in compassion born of wisdom, Buddhism temporarily acknowledges the individual self in order to point out to it the truth – that it has arisen on the basis of an incomplete assessment of what is self and what is not-self. It does not arise unconditionally, but on a foundation of original unity that has divided into two activities, but not into real, separate entities.

But how do these two activities give rise to an apparent "I am" self; how is it that this unified foundation "opens" into this world? Roshi explains that the foundation, the source, is actually composed of these two activities and that it is in their very nature to separate and unify repeatedly. When they are unified, subject and object, plus and minus, are one. Roshi calls this the "Zero" state because when unified, there is no plus or minus – they have dissolved into the union. He goes on to explain that this unification is not a fixated state. It inevitably breaks apart because it is also in the nature of these activities to separate and oppose each other. When they do separate, a distance opens between them.

Roshi explains, "When they separate, plus and minus give an equal amount of themselves. And what appears, by receiving this tiny amount of plus and minus, is the distance which I have been talking about. This distance is a limited space, in contrast to the true cosmos, the (all-inclusive) empty space; this (distance) is an imperfect activity of emptiness which appears by limiting the empty space. This distance, this space, is the beginning of the "I am" self which all beings have; this is a teaching of Buddhism."

Roshi encourages us to recognize that what we are experiencing as the objective world in this moment is the tiniest portion (sometimes called .0000000001) of the minus principle, which is the infinity of manifestation. Likewise, what we are experiencing as the subjective world in this moment is the tiniest portion of the plus principle, which is the principle that manifests subjective experience throughout the infinity of manifestation. And Roshi says that the two always arise simultaneously and are unified at their origin.

Introduction to an Interview with Joshu Roshi

Just as when a husband and wife unite and separate a child is born, here too in the separation of the two activities, is a child (the "I am" self) born. This child resides in the apparent distance between the two principles. It looks at its "parents," the subjective world and the objective world, and perceives the subjective as being within and the objective as being without. This view is very radical for a self fixated only in the subjective position. The "I am" self cannot see the unified foundation from which it has arisen. It can only see the separated subjectified and objectified nature of the two activities.

Roshi repeats over and over again that this self we take ourselves to be, this individual self, is an "imperfect self," that every individual self is an imperfect self, and that the true nature of the individual self is the origin out of which it has emerged.

Roshi teaches that after the "I am" self is born, it takes up the activity of living, the expansion of the plus activity. The expansion of the plus activity inevitably culminates in the manifestation of the "ultimate large" world, as Roshi describes it. The self, at that point, realizes that everything which arises in the entire cosmos is arising as one with it. Roshi calls this a state in which the plus can no longer expand, and subject and object, husband and wife, are unified. Roshi also notes that this is a state without any trace of the activity of mind.

It is a state "beyond comparison" and "of perfect rest" because there is nothing outside of it, there is nothing existing but it. Roshi also calls this state the "true God" and the "manifestation of True Love." In the human world individuals seek the perfection of love with the beloved. The "ultimate large" is that actual union.

But this, too, is not a fixated state. This state breaks apart as subject and object again separate and oppose each other. However, a new kind of subject, a new kind of husband, emerges from the experience of "ultimate large." This husband, although not in the experience of the union of subject and object, nevertheless gazes back on the union and knows that his wife (the objective universe), although now appearing at a distance, is originally one with him. Roshi describes, with beautiful imagery, how the wife now takes the lead and the husband follows. After the experience of union with his wife, the will of the husband is to flow with life, completely flexible to circumstances (wife), knowing that she is the manifestation of the ultimate.

Roshi notes that after the experience of the "ultimate large" world, there is no further need for or meaning to self affirmation, or the activity of living. The foundation of the "I am" self is known. The husband then follows his wife back to the source and realizes there is no need to perform the dying activity either. In other words, there is no need to practice negating the self because the self is fundamentally empty.

This brief summary of Roshi's teachings is presented to assist with following the extraordinary ideas and imagery in the interview.

Please enjoy this wonderful opportunity to reflect on life through the teachings of a master.

THE INTERVIEW

Introduction to an Interview with Joshu Roshi

ROSHI'S ZEN TEACHINGS

 THE FIRST DAY

ROSHI | I heard you have things to ask me – you would like to write my biography. But there is no biography in my life – I would like to address this at the beginning.

Originally I had the idea that an interview about your life would be central for this album, but after thinking about it, it seemed a waste of your time to discuss your personal history. I would like to ask Roshi instead to elaborate on his teachings. It is my hope he will agree to this kind of interview.

ROSHI | That's fine. You have been studying zazen with me. If you ask me from your own understanding of Buddhism, I would answer your questions. That's fine.

Well, the purpose of questions would be twofold: to ask questions and also to provide a vehicle for Roshi to speak.

ROSHI | Yes.

And also before starting I want to thank Roshi for agreeing to do this and taking so much time. So, the first question is: what is Roshi? And what does he see and know that ordinary humans do not see and know?

ROSHI | Difficult question. Asking any question comes from where? If a self did not arise, no questions would bubble up either, would they? What do you think?

Because we were delivered into this world, we must live. However, if we overlook the nature of our delivery into this world, our being born, without knowing where this activity of mind comes from, it is difficult to ask real questions. Therefore, I am wondering if the questioner is realizing that the one who asks the question is myself, if this person is really studying Zen.

"Roshi" is a title in the world of Zen, a term of endearment, a name, which means "old person." And that Roshi has nothing different; he was born by meeting the activity of being born just like everybody else. There are two ways of looking at birth, two ways of thinking about our own birth. One is to meet the activity of delivery and the other is to meet the activity of being born. Needless to say, when we say "I am born," we must ask "Who delivered me?" This may seem like something trivial, but it is a very profound thing.

If one were asked, "Who are your parents?" everybody would

answer, "My parents are my father and my mother." If we deepen this idea, a person who studies religion will think those parents are God, or a vehicle for God. Perhaps it is resolved in this way: although my father and mother are my parents, those parents are also God. So, such a person would think we are connected to God even at our birth and throughout the rest of life.

What is Roshi referring to by the term "God?"

ROSHI | It is coming gradually. How does the questioner think about God? I have just said now, being born from God is one way of thinking. This is the idea that God and self are directly connected. What is God? Since one is directly connected to God, we can think only that we were given our birth by God. If we were to expand on this idea, the inquiry would follow thus: "In what type of activity would God engage him/herself to accomplish the activity of delivery?" So, is your question solved?

I am assuming that by "God," you are not assuming a separate being?

ROSHI | If there is an idea that God and oneself are directly connected, we have to think what kind of relationship does this self have with God? It is not good to acknowledge God unconditionally. Everyone acknowledges God unconditionally, which is absolutely incorrect from the Buddhist point of view. What is God? When we examine the issue of God and self – if we think God and self are directly connected – this is fine. However, other answers acknowledge God unconditionally.

If we say "directly connected," it is by performing the activity of "directly connected." When God and oneself are directly connected, there is no other way to answer except to say "directly connected." If the person does not have the idea of being directly connected, there would be other ideas such as "God is love," or "God is something. . . ." Therefore, besides the answer of "We are directly connected to God,"all other answers acknowledge the activity of mind unconditionally, which Buddhism strongly criticizes. People tend to acknowledge the activity of mind unconditionally and start talking this and that immediately.

Although human beings are directly connected to God, there are occasions of being away from God and standing in the state of human beings. That happens after the "I am" self is born. As long as the "I am" self is not born, we are directly connected to God. Therefore, Buddhism says that when one is separated from God, the state of human being occurs.

Perhaps people wonder how God gives rise to the state of human being? Since God is the absolute being, God never brings external materials to create children. If God brings materials to create children or to create a place of living, it is not a true act of God. Buddhism teaches us that God creates children by dividing into two.

> Although human beings are directly connected to God, there are occasions of being away from God and standing in the state of human beings. That happens after the "I am" self is born. As long as the "I am" self is not born, we are directly connected to God.

I KNOW YOU ARE TRYING REALLY HARD IN YOUR ZAZEN, AND YOU ARE CRYING AND I AM CRYING, AND IT IS GREAT THAT YOU ARE TRYING HARD, BUT YOU ARE STILL STUCK IN YOUR FLAT WAY OF DOING ZAZEN. YOU ARE BEING EMBRACED FROM THE INSIDE AND FROM THE OUTSIDE — YOU MUST REALIZE THIS SPHERICAL ZAZEN. YOU CANNOT REALIZE THIS IF YOU ARE ATTACHED TO YOUR TWO-DIMENSIONAL WAY OF THINKING.

The 100th Year of Joshu Sasaki Roshi

Here comes another question: what is dividing into two when God divides itself? The absolute being – God – already contains within itself the two activities. Then, the idea "I was delivered from God" and the idea "I was born from God" and the fact that two opposing activities created me – all these become the same idea. It is a difficult point and it is fine for questions to come up. If you have questions, ask me please.

> Would it be correct to say that one way of describing the difference between Roshi and human beings is that what human beings take most pride in and draw meaning from – assuming their own independent existence – Roshi sees as the obstruction of the original communion with absolute being, with "God?" So for human beings ego is the source of great pride, whereas for Roshi ego is a painful thing because it signifies separation from God?

ROSHI | Such an idea is drawn after studying "a child is born after God divides itself into two" much deeper. It is a bit too soon for that. My response has not gone that far. What I am saying now is that a self has an activity of mind behind it.

First I wish to talk about the self which is born, or delivered – what kind of process it goes through to grow and develop. Everybody has practiced such a process, however people tend to claim an "I am" self without realizing that. That causes troubles. The teaching of Buddhism is that the self which is born will inevitably grow and develop without fixation. At this point we have to study carefully this growth and development and ask what the true way of existence is. Are you with me? May I continue talking?

> Would the following example make a good comparison? If someone came over to you and said, "I would like to have a dream, but I don't know how. Please explain to me how I could have a dream." And you say to that person, "Well, in order for you to have a dream, you have to divide yourself into two, so that there is a self who is appearing to have objective experiences." Is this an accurate metaphor for what Roshi is referring to?

ROSHI | That itself is like a dream tale. Surely the way of human existence is like a dream tale. That is surely so. The way of human existence is all non-fixated, all like a dream. That is why it is often said, "*Yume no gotoshi*" (like a dream). Human beings think this *Yume no gotoshi* is real and want to write it down. Wanting to record dreams – that is the way of human beings. No matter how many records they make, their records never become real. Inevitably they wake up and realize, "Oh, I was dreaming." Inevitably they wake up from their dreams, or inevitably they forget their dreams. As soon as they wake up, they are already forgetting their dreams. The dreams are surely only dreams, not real.

Therefore, our meeting here together is also like a dream. Inevitably we will be apart again.

> Human beings think this *Yume no gotoshi* is real and want to write it down. Wanting to record dreams – that is the way of human beings. No matter how many records they make, their records never become real. Inevitably they wake up and realize, "Oh, I was dreaming."

Everybody sees dreams. Whether good dreams or bad dreams, everybody knows dreams are only dreams and not real. There may be some people who think dreams are somehow real because we hear "good dreams" and "bad dreams." But dreams always disappear.

> There are people who get paid $250 an hour to tell others what their dreams mean.

ROSHI | That's fine! That's like a dream. Have dreams and receive $250 – it is neither heavy nor light. That's like a dream tale. Buddhism also takes up having dreams. Everybody dreams. When we are tired and sleep deeply, we don't dream. It is a mischievous activity of mind. While we are asleep, an activity of mind occurs, this is a dream. It is not real, and that is what Buddhism teaches. Talking about dreams requires a long time because psychology is popular now. However while Buddhism acknowledges dreams, it regards dreams as not true activities of mind. And even true activities of mind are dream-like.

It takes time, but if you practice, you will gradually understand that everybody dreams, but dreams are not real. So, Buddhism concludes that human beings are also like a dream. The self which was born – the fact that I was born, is true. But, no matter how this self attaches to the activity of living, the state of living will never become fixated in the activity of living.

The question then arises: what kind of activity is the living activity and what kind of activity is the dying activity? As I mentioned earlier, God is that which contains both the plus activity and the minus activity. In God, the plus and minus are unified in the true and perfect state. It is the state of neither plus nor minus; it is called the state of Zero, the perfect state in Buddhism. This perfect state is the manifestation of plus and minus being unified. It is also called the manifestation of the activity of *ku* (emptiness). An example of such a perfect state in the human world would be the happily married couple, although, of course, there is no need to be married to know this state.

Therefore, the teaching says that the state of the married couple and the state of the individual are different but the same. The state of a married couple is *Hin-Ju-Ittai** (the unification of object and subject). The teachings say that object and subject inevitably manifest the state of unification, but again, just as inevitably, this unification manifests the state of separation without fixation. When plus and minus are unified, they are perfect – they have the perfect activity. And when these plus and minus activities are in perfect union, the world does not exist and individual beings do not exist.

Only this is the perfect state, only this *Hin-Ju-Ittai* is truth – that is what the teaching temporarily tells us. The teaching says that the manifestation of unification is the activity of plus experiencing and containing minus, and, on the other

---

* Translator's note: in this expression of Chinese characters, *hin* means "an object," *ju* (*shu*) means "a subject."
Ichi : one + *tai* : body = *ittai* "one body, unification."

hand, the activity of minus experiencing and containing plus.

In the human world we can see times when a state of unification is broken suddenly. It gives rise to sadness and sorrow. However, in truth, it is not necessary to be sad. Why? When plus and minus are separated, the world, which is the distance between plus and minus, *inevitably* appears. The distance is the origin of all beings, according to Buddhism. When plus and minus are opposed and separated from each other, a distance appears in between; and, at the same time the distance appears between them, what we call father and mother appear as that which will close the distance simultaneously. Therefore, it is possible that even though plus and minus are separated, the child – the "I am" self – is not born, and they are not manifesting the true *Hin-Ju-Bunri** (the separation of object and subject); they are still manifesting the *Hin-Ju-Ittai* (the unification of object and subject).

When *Hin-Ju-Bunri* appears, it is the same as saying the separation of plus and minus appears. When they separate, plus and minus give an equal amount of themselves. And what appears, by receiving this tiny amount of plus and minus, is the distance which I have been talking about. This distance, in contrast to the true cosmos, the all-inclusive empty space, is a limited space. It is an imperfect activity of emptiness which appears by limiting the empty space. This distance, this space, is the beginning of the "I am" self which all beings have; this is a teaching of Buddhism.

As mentioned earlier, at the same time that the incomplete space, the distance, appears, the father and the mother appear. You can see how terrifying and incorrect the teachings are which tell people that beings are born from parents unconditionally.

Is there time for a question? I don't want to break the line of thought though.

ROSHI | Fine, fine. When it is cut, that means a new activity of mind is born. So, that's fine.

In the state of union of subject and object, can that also be called the state of no mental activity, completely without thinking? That is one question.

ROSHI | At the moment of *Hin-Ju-Ittai*, both object and subject are unified, aren't they? Beside that, what else is there? There isn't anything. So, I am telling you now, at the moment of *Hin-Ju-Ittai*, the world of separation disappears; it doesn't exist. By the activity of *Hin-Ju-Bunri*, the father, the mother and the "I am" self all appear simultaneously. And the teaching tells us they appear as the worlds which are called past, present and future. And those past, present and future worlds are not fixated – inevitably they will disappear into the world of Zero.

One more question please: If a practitioner of Zen is trying to realize the union of subject and object, the only

* *bun* : separate, divide +
  ri : distance =
  bunri : separation

possible way would be to completely negate his/her own mental activity – which breaks the prior union of subject and object – would that be accurate? If someone is practicing zazen trying to realize the state of the union of self and cosmos, would the path to enter that state have to be the death or dissolution of the mental activity of the practitioner?

ROSHI | It is not good enough to try to annihilate, it just disappears. When your husband calls you, "Honey!" what are you thinking? Do you understand? When your husband calls you, "Honey!" you would not think anything. This is *Hin-Ju-Ittai*. "Honey!" – "Uh!" See, the distance has disappeared! You tilt your head because you are still attached to the activity of mind. It is not good to attach to the activity of mind. The way of a married couple does not have attachments; it is completely free. Always a new self appears. There are two aspects in this new self. One is the self which appears by *Hin-Ju-Ittai* and the other self appears by *Hin-Ju-Bunri*. Shake your hand with your husband's. See, the new self appeared. Then, you say, "Honey, be well, bye-bye!" See, the new self appears again. Zen teaches that a new self is always continuously appearing.

Everybody studies while too much attached to the activity of mind, which, by itself, is fine. However, they are attached to the activity of mind. When husband and wife shake their hands, they don't need to attach to anything. In the same way, when they say goodbye, they both agree and have the same activity of mind for them to be apart. In either case, they aren't attached. However, when they have to be apart without agreement, they are sad. Surely there will be such occasions, but they are also like dreams; inevitably they will be apart and a new self will appear. Therefore, it is quite natural for the couple to be sad when they face separation all of a sudden. Everybody would be sad on such occasions. However, understanding the principle of "being apart yet not separated," one is no longer saddened. When the activity of mind which understands the principle of "being apart yet not separated" appears, the person does not experience sadness on the occasion of being apart. That is something difficult; it is like a dream. Did you have another question?

Can Roshi speak more about how the "I am" self is born in this way . . . ?

ROSHI | This part is very difficult to understand, it takes many years of practice to grasp. It is impossible with only a little practice. It is like a dream.

Well, I would like to continue with this principle. You will understand clearly in its course. Is it OK to proceed?

So, we are continuously repeating the states of *Hin-Ju-Bunri* and *Hin-Ju-Ittai* and manifesting those repeatedly. Buddhism has a special term, *genzen,* meaning manifestation. If you study the manifestation of a new self well enough, you will understand the principle of repetition of *Hin-Ju-Bunri* and *Hin-Ju-Ittai*.

The manifestation of *ku* (emptiness) or Zero is the unified state of plus and minus. The teaching of Tathagata Zen says we have to study this very carefully. When a foundation divides itself, it eventually manifests a new foundation. What kind of activity appears in its course? Inevitably we find the repetition *of Hin-Ju-Bunri* and *Hin-Ju-Ittai*. By going through such a repeated process, a new state of the foundation is eventually manifested. To explain it in greater detail, the state of the foundation is the state of Zero in which plus and minus appear unified. The imperfect self, the "I am" self, does not exist in this state. In such a state the sequential past, present and future disappear; in their place appears the manifestation of perfect time, eternity, one could say. Buddhism teaches that the state of the foundation is the manifestation of perfect time and it is something profound.

Now, when this foundation manifests a new foundation, a secondary foundation, it inevitably goes through the process of manifestation of *Hin-Ju-Bunri* and *Hin-Ju-Ittai*, and subsequently this new secondary foundation will appear, according to the teaching. *(Please translate this part carefully without any mistake!)* In the process of manifesting the secondary foundation, inevitably the state of the foundation manifests the worlds of past, present and future. Then it manifests the

> A *koan* appears: "When you see a flower, where is God?" Although this koan may be given to beginner students of Zen, it is a very difficult koan for them. When one sees a flower, one devotes love to the flower and subsequently manifests unification; surely any Roshi would teach so.

world of *Hin-Ju-Ittai* where the worlds of past, present and future disappear. It is the very nature of the activity of plus and minus to alternately manifest *Hin-Ju-Bunri* and *Hin-Ju-Ittai*, and to culminate in manifesting the state *of Hin-Ju-Ittai*.

A *koan* appears: "When you see a flower, where is God?" Although this *koan* may be given to beginner students of Zen, it is a very difficult *koan* for them. When one sees a flower, one devotes love to the flower and subsequently manifests unification; surely any Roshi would teach so.

In such a process *Hin-Ju* (object and subject) are unified. When plus and minus are unified completely, the former world of *Hin-Ju-Bunri* disappears completely and a secondary foundation appears. The former world is truly like a dream. Although we often say "the state of the foundation," "the state of the foundation" is not fixated. If we consider the existence of God in anthropomorphic terms, we would say God is never a fixated state or a fixated being; God will inevitably manifest a new secondary foundation; this is what Buddhism teaches. So, now I have briefly explained the process of the foundation manifesting a secondary foundation, yet so many things happen in this process in reality.

Is it correct to say that out of the state of the foundation, a certain wisdom appears which reflects back on the state of unification and knows that the state of separation of subject and object is dreamlike? Would that be accurate?

ROSHI | The state of the foundation is the foundation of all manifestation – it appears having the activity of containing everything within. Therefore, the state of foundation turns out to be the manifestation of True Love. And later, Buddhism says this state of foundation has two aspects. Difficult, isn't it? Why so? Because when the plus performs actively, the state of *GokuDai* (ultimate large) inevitably appears. This is difficult, so I will touch on it just a little bit. The manifestation of *GokuDai* is, needless to say, "ultimate large," so this is the manifestation of the result of plus expressing "there is no necessity of becoming large any more."

The opposite aspect has the manifestation of *GokuDai* as its foundation, and has the activity of going back to the state of *GokuShou* (ultimate small). By manifesting the contraction, it will inevitably manifest the state which does not need to contract any more; this is the teaching of Buddhism. Let me repeat again. The teaching says that when the plus performs actively, without fail it will inevitably manifest the state of *GokuDai* in which it realizes, "I cannot have any more activity of expansion than this. There is no necessity of becoming larger any more." Having such a manifestation of *GokuDai* as its foundation, the activity of minus performs the contrary function, which inevitably manifests this cosmos as the state of *GokuShou*, which says, "There is no necessity of becoming smaller than this."

Just to clarify, when Roshi talks about the "ultimately large," does he mean that the self realizes it is one with everything, one with space, one with time, one with every possible manifestation, it is "ultimately large," cannot be larger, one with everything that has appeared, can appear, and will appear – is that what is meant?

ROSHI | Of course. Since it is *GokuDai*, this is the state which appears as embracing everything. When plus activity reaches the manifestation of *GokuDai*, it is the state in which plus activity does not need to have the activity of plus, the activity of expansion; this is the manifestation of *GokuDai*. If some opinion would arise at this point, perhaps Roshi would hit the speaker with a stick, saying "Idiot!" If it were Rinzai saying so, he would hit saying, "You are still attached to the activity of mind! You, such an idiot!" and then the student would wake up for the first time.

When manifesting the activity of *ku* – the activity of Zero, the "I am," which is the imperfect self, completely vanishes. Reaching this point, Buddhism says that the wife thinks for the first time, "My husband is myself. He is not my husband but myself." Therefore, when one says – "my husband," "my wife" – one's thinking is immature. The activity of mind "my husband is myself" inevitably appears and is called in Buddhism *KanzenChi no Genzen** (the manifestation of perfect wisdom). Inevitably, the imperfect self, the "I am," disappears and manifests, in union with his wife, the state in

* *Kanzen* means "perfect," *chi* in this context is the same as *chie*, which Roshi-sama also often uses, and means "wisdom" and *no* is a particle which has the same function as "of" in English.

> If some opinion would arise at this point, perhaps Roshi would hit the speaker with a stick, saying "Idiot!" If it were Rinzai saying so, he would hit saying, "You are still attached to the activity of mind! You, such an idiot!" and then the student would wake up for the first time.

which the activity of expansion of plus is no longer possible.

As I just mentioned, the activity of mind "my husband is myself" inevitably appears, and that is taught as the manifestation of *KanzenChi, Maka Hannya Haramita, Hannya no Chi** in Buddhism. Although I am going to elaborate on this later, the teaching tells us that, in the manifestation of perfect wisdom, plus is perfectly manifesting *GokuDai* with minus. Although plus and minus are always opposed to each other, the wife inevitably helps her husband's activity of manifesting *GokuDai,* and by this support from his wife the husband manifests *GokuDai*. If this principle is not clear, people get lost wondering what life is all about. Buddhism teaches us that inevitably the wife helps the husband and the husband manifests *GokuDai* with his wife.

Would Roshi prefer to continue, or would a new question be better?

ROSHI | A new question would be better so that Roshi can see what kind of activity of mind you have.

If not one person appears who understands my teaching – either through practice or concepts – then Rinzai-ji will become chaotic; if one person understands, not necessarily through practice but even only through words, it would be all right; but if nobody understands, either by practice or by words, Rinzai-ji will be chaotic.

Since you said that you will write Roshi's Zen, I will talk to you as if Roshi himself is writing these teachings.

> Roshi has said that after the experience of ultimate expansion, a new kind of self arises that practices dying until dying does not need to be done anymore. Can Roshi please elaborate on that idea? When Roshi says a self arises, does Roshi mean a new state of mind arises that realizes that there is nothing more to be experienced because insight into the ultimate nature has arisen?

ROSHI | Always, always a new self appears. If a new self would not appear, if a new state of mind would not appear, how would you know what you are doing?

I am going to talk now. I would like to review what we have spoken of.

Temporarily acknowledging the two opposing activities and having that acknowledgment study the nature of life – that is Buddhism, that is the Buddhist approach. The opposing two activities, the plus and minus activities, are they fixated? No, they are not. These plus and minus activities unify and separate repeatedly.

Buddhism teaches that the state of the foundation has two manifestations, "ultimate large" – a state beyond comparison,

---

* All three expressions can be translated as "Perfect Wisdom," which is the translation of the Sanskrit term, *maha prajna paramita*. If I were to try to explain the differences, *Kanzen-Chi* is the same expression in vernacular Japanese; *Maka Hannya Haramita* is the Japanese reading of the sutra in Chinese; *Hannya no Chi* is a Buddhist term in Japanese.

and "ultimate small," and both of them are truth. The "ultimate large" is one truth and the "ultimate small" is one truth and they alternate and repeat. When the nature of being is taught, the first step is to teach this state of the foundation which includes everything.

There are two activities that become active within the foundation – the plus activity and the minus activity. The perfect state is the unification of the plus and minus activities. That state appears when the "I am" self disappears. In the teachings, it says that the foundation of the plus and minus activities is the unification of the plus and minus activities. We can also say it this way: The plus god and the minus god are unified, and this is the True God.

This temporary teaching tells us that in the state of the foundation, the plus and minus become opposed to each other and then unify repeatedly. This is happening very actively. This teaching says that there appears a pregnancy which gives birth to time and to children – all sentient beings. This is a difficult and important point – the children are not born unconditionally. The foundation has manifested the activity of being pregnant and meets the activity of time which gives birth to a child – existence. To give birth to existence means that the activities of plus and minus oppose each other and then separate from each other.

Although the foundation is unified, after the separation there is the manifestation of three worlds – past, present and future. Because people affirm the activity of mind unconditionally and stand in the "I am" self as if it were fixated, no matter how many times I explain this activity, even if I tell you millions of times, you cannot understand. The activity of mind is born simultaneously when the self is born. However, it is the foundation that has manifested the self. The state of the foundation has manifested the state of being pregnant and only after that, for the first time, the "I am" self appears.

> Just to review: When Roshi says that the "I am" self does not arise unconditionally, is it meant that in truth, it arises on the basis of the ultimate union of subject and object but that it is thinking of itself on the basis of being only the subject, that it is arising in ignorance because it is arising out of a union with everything, but it is not thinking on that basis? Is this a correct stating of what Roshi means?

ROSHI | After the unified subject and object break apart, this "I am" self appears, but this is really only the activity of mind. For human beings there is a habit to acknowledge the "I am" self, which is only an activity of mind, so we have to be very careful. *PON!* – when you hear this sound, what kind of activity of mind do you have? There is a *koan* like that. When the wife calls her husband, "Honey!" what kind of activity of mind occurs? As I mentioned earlier, when you see a flower, what kind of activity of mind do you have? If you

> Because people affirm the activity of mind unconditionally and stand in the "I am" self as if it were fixated, no matter how many times I explain this activity, even if I tell you millions of times, you cannot understand. The activity of mind is born simultaneously when the self is born.

practiced with these *koans* again and again, you would understand why and how the activity of mind occurs.

The relationship of the husband and wife is also the activity of mind. When the husband and wife have to be separated suddenly, both will be very sad because the place of their practice of the activity of mind will disappear. Whether they are separated or whether they are unified – in both cases it is the activity of mind that appears. Either way, they are in the one world. If you understand the principle of being separated, then even if you are separated from your wife, you know that you are living in one world. So this is a really difficult thing – even if you are separated, you are not separated. It is difficult to attain such wisdom. The person who understands that even if we are separated, we are not separated – such a person is very developed.

The *Heart Sutra* says, "Doesn't increase, doesn't decrease" – even if we are separated, we are still together in one world. Saying this means that the self does not grow and does not develop. Inevitably, one realizes that there is no activity of dying and no activity of living. Buddhism teaches us that in the manifestation of the "ultimate large," there is no necessity to have the activity of living, and in the manifestation of "ultimate small," there is no necessity of having the activity of dying. If you have attached to mind, it is really difficult to understand. Dying is really a big deal. However, this activity of dying and the activity of living disappear in this one world. It seems difficult, but if you think carefully, it is not difficult because we are all living in this one world. OK?

The interview continues on page 34

Walking the 100th Year

April 1 – 7, 2006	Rinzai-ji Dai-Sesshin
April 28	Jemez Bodhi Manda Kessei begins
April 30 – May 6	Dai Sesshin
May 21 – 27	Dai-Sesshin
May 28	Jemez Bodhi Manda Kessei ends
June 5 – 16	Seminar on the Sutras at Bodhi
June 22 – 28	Rinzai-ji Dai-Sesshin
July 3	Mount Baldy Summer Seichu begins
July 12 – 18	Dai Sesshin
July 23 – 29	Rinzai-ji Dai-Sesshin
August 6 – 11	Dai-Sesshin
September 3 – 9	Dai-Sesshin
September 13	Mount Baldy Summer Seichu ends
Sept. 28 – October 4	Rinzai-ji Dai-Sesshin
October 13 – 15	Haku-un-ji Weekend Sesshin
October 17	Jemez Bodhi Manda Kessei begins
October 22 – 29	Dai-Sesshin
November 5 – 11	Dai-Sesshin
November 23 – 29	Rohatsu Dai-Sesshin
November 30	Jemez Bodhi Manda Kessei ends
December 9	Mount Baldy Winter Seichu begins
December 15 – 22	Rohatsu Dai-Sesshin
January 11 – 17	Dai-Sesshin
January 24 – 30	Rinzai-ji Dai-Sesshin
February 8 – 14	Dai-Sesshin
February 25 – March 3	Dai-Sesshin
March 5	Seichu ends
March 9 – 11	Haku-un-ji Weekend Sesshin
March 17 – 24	Puerto Rico Dai-Sesshin
April 1 – 7	Rinzai-ji Dai-Sesshin
April 8	Roshi's 100TH birthday celebration

The 100th Year of Joshu Sasaki Roshi

ROSHI'S ZEN TEACHINGS

THE SECOND DAY

Yesterday, when we finished we were talking about the activity of dying, that after realizing the state of "ultimate large," a self arises that realizes it must practice the activity of dying until manifesting the "ultimate small." Can Roshi please go over that?

ROSHI | Buddhism acknowledges two opposing activities. When we practice or think about why we are born from the point of view of the practice, if we don't acknowledge these two opposing activities, we cannot answer correctly and we cannot realize the manifestation of "ultimate large."

The teaching tells us that these two activities of plus and minus start simultaneously – one never arises without the other – they are always simultaneous. However, although they are simultaneous, there are differences in how they function. When plus starts moving, minus follows. However, this teaching is for people who unconditionally acknowledge the activity of mind. That is why Buddhism teaches that plus is a little forward moving and minus follows.

Would Roshi prefer just to speak or is it all right to ask questions?

ROSHI | Questions are all right.

I am trying to have a practical understanding of what Roshi is saying. For example when Roshi says the plus activity moves and the minus follows, is this referring to, in simple terms, if we hear the sound *PON!* simultaneously the receptor becomes *PON!*? When I see a flower, it is because my self has become that flower. Is this what Roshi means by the "plus and minus moving together," or is Roshi speaking of something completely different?

ROSHI | Very different. Take a mother and a child. When the child breathes, the mother immediately knows the child is healthy. If the husband says *Ha*, the wife immediately catches that *Ha*. When the plus says *Ha*, the minus immediately catches it. So there is no separation, even though there is a space in between. So, saying "Later on," or, "A little bit later on," implies a distance and that is an arrogant activity of mind. When the mother says *Ha*, the child immediately catches it. When there are two things, there is air in between and the distance is the air itself. The air is mixing the two activities. If there is no air, no separation, there would be no problem. But if there is separation, there would be a problem. The *Heart Sutra* says *mu shiki*, "no form" – there is no material – this is *mu shiki*. The teaching says that the child and the mother are limiting the air.

When the husband and wife are apart, there is a worry – the cosmos is between them. The husband and wife are limiting the space, and the things in between them are limited as well. Distance appears by limiting the entire cosmos, the space. This is really difficult – many questions come up when a person has unconditional activity of mind. The relationship between mother and child is very difficult for people who acknowledge their "I am" self unconditionally. But, fundamentally, there is no "I am" self in the true state.

When plus and minus have their true relationship, there is no activity of mind. However, when plus and minus oppose each other and are in the state of separation, distance appears, and at that time, both of them have the "I am" self. The self which was born **is** the distance between them. The same holds with the husband and wife situation. Asking what kind of place is it where the activity of mind appears is a good question. I would answer that because there is a separation, the child, which is distance, appears. At that time the parents and child, all three of them, have the activity of mind. I can answer this way when one asks what place is it where the activity of mind is born.

If one were to ask what kind of situation is it in which the activity of mind appears? Does the "I am" self appear first and then the activity of mind? Or does the activity of mind appear before the birth of the "I am" self? Such a question is difficult for me to answer. Activity of mind appears after the plus and minus have a relationship. This is what Buddhism teaches us.

Buddhism also says that the activity of mind does not arise if plus and minus do not have a relationship, if plus and minus are not separate. There is no thinking when husband and wife are deeply in love – there are no questions when you are deeply in love. However, when the wife escapes from the husband, the husband thinks – where are you? And both of them are limited. Then each of them unconditionally

> When plus and minus oppose each other and are in the state of separation, distance appears, and at that time, both of them have the "I am" self. The self which was born **is** the distance between them.

holds the other again in love and both of them disappear. And the state of Zero appears – this is the teaching. Tinier than the tiniest is the manifestation of love. In the state of unification, there is no front, no back, no inside, no outside.

When they are separated, both of them are limiting the source. The imperfect world appears as the distance between husband and wife. And then they meet again and manifest zero. Without this meeting there would be no appearance of the *Prajna Paramita*, which is the perfect wisdom.

The human way of thinking is not the *Prajna Paramita*, the perfection of wisdom. This is a difficult point. If you can see this, your Zen practice is mature. If you wander around in the activity of mind, then you are lost.

> The desire to practice with great passion to gain insight into the fundamental principle – what is it that gives rise to this passion? What causes a student to show up so motivated to practice?

ROSHI | If you are attached to the activity of mind, then the wife or the husband will come up and hit you *Boom!* And then you realize, "Oh, that's right!" and then you would apologize.

When I see how people are holding on to their religions, it is clear why there is never peace in this world. When I see the leaders in this world making war in the name of religion,

The 100th Year of Joshu Sasaki Roshi

I want to hit them and say, "Wake up!" I listen to what the U.S. is doing and it is sad to stand so fixated in a particular religion.

The perfect activity of mind has no "I am" self. When the husband and wife quarrel, they separate. But then later, they lose the "I am" self again.

> Roshi has said that the purpose of Zen practice is to realize "no self" and to manifest a life in accordance with the principle of "no self." What is the nature of a life manifested in accordance with "no self?"

ROSHI | The nature of things is never that way. Nature would never make a mistake. Nature inevitably negates the "I am" self. If we don't negate the "I am" self, we would never taste the true flavor of married life. How would the wife recognize the husband? How would the husband recognize the wife?

There are many *koans* about this point. And many students try to answer these *koans*, but I cannot accept their answers because the only true answer is – "This is me! This is myself!" If a husband and wife cannot recognize that the other is oneself, then this marriage will not last very long. When the wife thinks, "My husband is myself," there is calmness and peace. If the husband thinks, "My wife is myself," the husband is perfect.

When the husband goes out into the desert because he cannot find his wife, he will suffer loneliness and sorrow until he is able to realize himself. There is no one around. How can he realize his self? This is a *koan*.

Breaking through that point, for the first time he realizes his true nature which is true love.

> Would it be a correct understanding to say that what ordinary people attribute to will, from Roshi's perspective, since there is ultimately no "I am" self, can be attributed to the will-less activity of the dharma? Are the choices and responses that people make to life simply like the grass growing in the sun – willess activity? Are people running this way and that way simply like leaves blowing in the wind?

ROSHI | The activity of nature is the activity of dharma. All things have the plus and minus activities as their content. Even the sun, shining through the window, is like this. The sun is not the sun. The sun is myself – this is very powerful. Nothing any religion can teach can have the power of this wisdom – the sun is myself.

Therefore, Buddhism is not Buddhism. If there is Buddhism, there will be religious war. I used to like President Bush. It would be good if he could learn about true religion so the conflict in the Middle East could be dissolved. Somewhere in his religion he is attached to a one-sided view and it has placed the United States in danger. When politicians with ambitions abuse their power to advance selfish policies, there

> There are many *koans* about this point. And many students try to answer these *koans,* but I cannot accept their answers because the only true answer is – "This is me! This is myself!"

> In this one world an imperfect self appears in the distance between them. However, inevitably there will be a re-unification of subject and object and the perfect world re-appears, and the manifestation of true love appears. And so it is essential for us to study the unification and separation of plus and minus very carefully until we can manifest it. Buddhism teaches us this.

is danger. It is not good for the president of the United States to be attached to a particular religion. It would be much better if he were on the path of practicing true democracy.

All of us who were born have to take up the activity of living. That is our duty. And it is our duty to reach the manifestation of the "ultimate large." Buddhism teaches us that we will reach a point when we no longer need to have the activity of living. And Buddhism also tells us that married life, the perfect union, the manifestation of the "ultimate large," will be profound. Those who realize the truth of married life, those people who realize the manifestation of perfection, those people attain the wisdom of the manifestation of the "ultimate large."

The teaching says that human activity will be the repetition of the unification and separation of subject and object for millions of times until the manifestation of the "ultimate large" appears and the perfect world appears. Whenever plus and minus separate, an imperfect world appears. In this one world an imperfect self appears in the distance between them. However, inevitably there will be a re-unification of subject and object and the perfect world re-appears, and the manifestation of true love appears. And so it is essential for us to study the unification and separation of plus and minus very carefully until we can manifest it. Buddhism teaches us this.

During this process, many worlds appear as the repetition of the unification and separation of subject and object repeats itself. If we compare these worlds, there are many differences in content. However, the *principle* of their manifestation is always the same – the separation and unification of subject and object. The rocks, mosquitoes, birds, human beings are all identical when it comes to the unification of the separation. If you do not understand this principle, you will be unable to comprehend the true activity of the mind.

However, when we examine the separation of subject and object, the worlds of birds and snakes are all different in their separated state. However, in the world of unification, all the beasts and humans, all of them manifest the perfect state. Therefore, the wisdom of knowing the nature of equality and distinction is what Buddhism teaches us. We must clearly grasp this principle. If we fail to do this, we will never have clear and correct insight into the nature of being human.

Ultimately, when the unification of subject and object has been repeated again and again, the ultimate knowledge appears. The husband, who has been very active until this point, when coming down from this height, takes out a handkerchief, wipes his brow and goes to sleep in the arms of his wife. The husband is in a state where he does not need any activity. But there is the activity of the wife, which is the contraction activity, and they return to the "ultimate small" as the wife desires to return to her source. Now the wife takes the lead and leads the husband back to her source. After the state of the "ultimate large," the husband wakes up, goes back to sleep and wakes up again until finally, with the help of the wife, for the first time, he awakens in satori – clearly awakened to the nature of things.

After the experience of the "ultimate large," the husband awakens with the realization that he must take up the activity of dying. The wife now takes the lead and the husband follows. After the world of "ultimate large" appears, the wife begins contracting in her journey back to the foundation, and the husband follows his wife, helping her on her return to the foundation. He must help her. And they reach the world of the "ultimate small" where there is no need to die anymore.

> The wisdom that comes forth from the appearance or manifestation of the world of the "ultimate large" is that the whole universe is illuminating as one, that the whole cosmos is oneself. What is the wisdom that comes forth from the world of the "ultimate small" when the self awakens?

ROSHI | It is the same thing. "Ultimate large" and "ultimate small" are both manifestations of the same thing. One self experiences the manifestation of "ultimate large" and "ultimate small." We have to grasp this conclusion clearly: one self is born to manifest this. This self may think, "I manifested the "ultimate large" so it is finished." However, the self cannot become fixated in that state.

The self realizes that the state of "ultimate large" requires the help of the wife, or union with the wife. After the "ultimate large," the wife is already doing the activity of going back to the "ultimate small." So the husband follows her and they die together and manifest the "ultimate small." This is the wisdom acquired. This is the activity of mind. Plus wakes up and thinks, "I must contain the activity of dying." All beings do not have the idea that they must contain the activity of dying and reach the "ultimate small" world – this idea has not yet arisen. Beings are always affirming themselves. The idea of holding and entering the dying activity together with the wife does not arise.

However, (after the manifestation of the "ultimate large") one realizes that dying together with the world and all the entities in this world is the true activity, and so husband and wife inevitably reach the "ultimate small." This, again, is the manifestation of true love. And in the same way, the manifestation of the "ultimate large" is the activity of true love. The two manifestations – the "ultimate large" and "ultimate small" – are the true manifestations of love. They are the manifestation of the perfect union of plus and minus, of husband and wife. That is the state which transcends the dying activity.

> The world of science is always asserting an objective world, but in Buddhism there is not any thing which is not one's self.

But this state is not fixated. Inevitably the activity of minus manifests the absence of the necessity of dying and the plus manifests its original activity without the necessity of dying – such a beautiful relationship. However, this "ultimate small" world is not fixated. The husband wakes up and resumes his original plus activity. And this is the foundation of the living activity. And then again plus and minus come together and separate until they enter into the manifestation of the "ultimate large" world together.

And then again from this "ultimate large" world, the plus gives rise to a self which realizes that it must manifest the dying activity. The wife realizes that inevitably she must return to her original place. And plus sacrifices itself to obey the activity of minus and helps his wife manifest the "ultimate small" together with him. And the original face appears at that time – when the husband sacrifices himself for the sake of his wife. If you understand this, you understand the state of our being, and this is what Buddhism is teaching us.

The plus is enlightened to the wisdom, "Everything is illuminating as myself. The "ultimate large" is the state that I reach together with my wife through the unification of subject and object – both are myself. My wife is appearing as the cosmos."

The world of science is always asserting an objective world, but in Buddhism there is not any thing which is not one's self.

This is why a husband kisses his wife or a mother her child. This is why in the airport a boyfriend and girlfriend kiss and embrace for a long, long time – because this is myself. To discover one's self is the purpose of Buddhism. So get married and have children and then separate from them and see how great the sadness is – no matter how much they cry, it is not enough. It requires a great deal of new wisdom to heal. A new self is suddenly born – then it allows us to break through such a difficult point and go forward. That knowledge is born that even if I am away from you, I am together with you in this one world. Until we die, although we are separated and I am away from you, we are still living in this one world together. And then the person has energy to go forward.

The people in the world compromise and then have a dream of peace. But if you compromise, you will never reach the real peace.

Everything is born from the foundation world. The original face of the foundation world – how does it open? The world of the foundation has no activity of mind, but it manifests the activity of mind, and through this activity it manifests both the living and dying activities. The foundation world also teaches us why the activity of mind appears.

The activity of mind is not denied. Buddhism temporarily acknowledges the activity of mind in order to teach us. The activity of mind manifests the "I am" self and such activity of mind is imperfect. The perfect activity of mind has no necessity to assert a self. To acknowledge the truth of this, and then to teach this, one has to have traveled a long path. We have traveled a long way and have gone through many processes to reach this point today. These processes are based in the activity of mind and we all experience these processes. However, these processes all disappear.

If we are captured by or attached to the activity of mind, we will not be able to experience the true self. When this activity of mind encounters the death activity, it will disappear. When the activity of mind dies – at that point – where is the self? It is the self that says, "This is the self, this is not the self, this flower is not me, these things are not me," and this death is difficult. But in conclusion, everything is self.

As I mentioned earlier, if someone goes to a foreign land or goes out into the desert, if that person cannot find the self, there will be sadness and loneliness. Just by discovering oneself, the person can be completely relieved. So how would that person find himself – without friends, family – how can that person find comfort and ease? Just by finding the self that knows "All this is myself," there is comfort and ease and the escape from sorrow.

IT IS A MIRACULOUS THING. UP UNTIL THEN YOU HAD THOUGHT A PINE TREE IS A PINE TREE; IT'S NOT ME. A BUG IS A BUG; IT'S NOT ME. GOD IS GOD; IT'S NOT ME. BUT WHEN WE PROPERLY SLEEP AND WAKE UP, WE REALIZE ALL BEINGS INHABIT ONE UNITED UNIVERSE. WHEN ONE'S EYES PROPERLY OPEN, ONE ENCOUNTERS A WONDERFUL, MIRACULOUS WORLD THAT IS BEYOND DESCRIPTION.

The moment I think that there are new people on Mount Baldy that want to PRACTICE with me, then I get energy, and even though it is farther away, it is easier for me to get there. Isn't it true that when you have a new lover, that it doesn't matter if it is pouring rain or howling wind, one way or another you will find a way to visit? Isn't it true that when your old lover is snoring in bed, you don't really want to stay there?

Rinzai-ji Oshos

During the forty-five years that Roshi has been teaching in America, thousands of students have come to practice with him. Some came and went while others stayed to immerse themselves in the dharma teachings and practice. They took up residence at Mount Baldy, Rinza-ji or Jemez Bodhi Manda to deepen their understanding, or they followed Roshi about as he taught. After a few years, they were ordained as monks or nuns as a sign of their commitment to the Buddhist way of life.

From among the monks and nuns, a few have taken up the life of sharing with others what they have experienced and learned. From Roshi they have received permission, through their ordination as Oshos (priests), to teach in their own situations or to assist in the management of Rinzai-ji and its temples.

The Osho Council is the official body of the oshos. The council meets several times per year, both to receive additional instruction from Joshu Roshi and to manage the many affairs of Rinzai-ji.

Roshi has ordained over twenty-five oshos and there are currently about forty Zen practicing communities in Rinzai-ji.

OSHOS ARE LISTED IN ORDER OF THEIR ORDINATION DATE

GISAN KODO RON OLSEN
  Monk ordination – 1964
  Osho ordination – 1972
  Joshu Zen Temple

KOZAN GENTEI SANDY STEWART
  Monk ordination – 1967
  Osho ordination – 1973
  North Carolina Zen Center

SEIUN GENRO HERBERT KOUDELA
  Monk ordination – 1973
  Osho ordination – 1975
  Bodhidharma Zendo Wien

SHOZAN MARC JOSLYN
  Monk ordination – 1972
  Osho ordination – 1982
  Little Zendo of Entsu-ji

KOGAN SEIJU BOB MAMMOSER
  Monk ordination – 1978
  Osho ordination – 1984
  Albuquerque Zen Center

TEKIO MICHAEL RADFORD
  Monk ordination – 1978
  Osho Ordination – 1986

HOON MYOSEN MARSHA OLSEN
  Nun ordination – 1976
  Osho ordination – 1988
  Joshu Zen Temple

HOJU ESHIN JOHN GODFREY
  Monk ordination – 1982
  Osho ordination – 1988
  Vancouver Zen Centre

JIUN HOSEN CHRISTIANE RANGER
  Nun ordination – 1983
  Osho ordination – 1988
  Jemez Bodhi Manda Zen Center

JIKO MYOKUN DIANNE SEGHESIO
  Nun ordination – 1984
  Osho ordination – 1988
  Myoko Ni Sorin

YOSHIN DAVID RADIN
  Monk ordination – 1983
  Osho ordination – 1989
  Ithaca Zen Center

ZUIUN GIKO DAVID RUBIN
  Monk ordination – 1983
  Osho ordination – 1999
  Kakusho-ji

JOZAN KOYO CHARLES ENGENNACH
  Monk ordination – 1984
  Osho ordination – 1999
  University Zen Center, Dai Gyo Ji

The 100th Year of Joshu Sasaki Roshi

ZENGETSU MYOKYO JUDITH MCLEAN
    Nun ordination – 1986
    Osho ordination – 1999
    Centre Zen de la Main, Enpuku-ji

HAKUUN SOKAI GEOFF BARRATT
    Monk ordination – 1987
    Osho ordination – 1999
    Haku-Un-Ji

UNGAN KIDO ERIC BERHOW
    Monk ordination – 1988
    Osho ordination – 1999
    Rokuon-ji

SEIGAKU KIGEN BILL EKESON
    Monk ordination – 1991
    Osho ordination – 1999
    Hollywood Zen Center

GAKUDO KOSHIN
CHRISTOPHER CAIN
    Monk ordination – 1991
    Osho ordination – 1999
    Puget Sound Zen Center

EKO CHERYL SCHNABEL
    Nun ordination – 1982
    Osho ordination – 2001
    Mt. Cobb Sai Sho Zen-ji

TOKUJU GENSHU CHRISTOPHER RO
    Monk ordination – 1988
    Osho ordination – 2001
    Williamsburg Zen Center

GIDO RICHARD SCHNABEL
    Monk ordination – 1996
    Osho ordination – 2001
    Mt. Cobb Sai Sho Zen-ji

KYOON DOKURO ROLAND JAECKEL
    Monk ordination – 1989
    Osho ordination – 2004
    Houn An Cambridge Buddhist Association

CHINZAN LES FEHMI
    Monk ordination – 1984
    Osho ordination – 2006
    Princeton Zen Society

GENSHIN EDGAR KANN
    Monk ordination – 1980
    Osho ordination – 2006
    Long Island Zen Center

DOAN BRUNO SCHABARUM
    Monk ordination – 1998
    Osho ordination – 2006

SEIDO LARRY CLARK
    Monk ordination – 1996
    Osho ordination – 2006
    Hogaku-ji Heki Un Zan

HOSEN, ROSHI, MYOKUN

Rinzai-ji Oshos

How should a self live?
It must have as its ideal to live life founded on the wisdom that all is one.

What most human beings are doing is fixating the self, identifying the "I am" self as the subject only, rather than seeing the complete or true self as the unification of subject and object.

That is why roshis have such short tempers and shout, "Don't give me your bull crap! Don't talk to me! Don't think anymore! Just kiss now!"

IN SANZEN, IF YOU CANNOT RESPOND WITH THE UNDERSTANDING THAT WHEN YOU SEE A FLOWER, YOU ARE LOOKING AT YOURSELF; WHEN YOU SEE A SNAKE, YOU ARE LOOKING AT YOURSELF; WHEN YOU SEE GOD, YOU ARE LOOKING AT YOURSELF — IF YOU CANNOT RESPOND WITH A SELF-GAZING RESPONSE, YOU ARE CUT IN TWO BY ROSHI. AND JUST LIKE A SNAKE THAT'S BEEN CUT, THE TWO PARTS ARE WRITHING AROUND IN AN UGLY WAY. IT IS MORE INTERESTING THAN WATCHING A MOVIE — *I FORGET HOW OLD I AM!*

48

The 100th Year of Joshu Sasaki Roshi

Rinzai-ji Temples and Centers

RINZAI-JI ZEN CENTER

Rinzai-ji Zen Center is the home and head temple for the Rinzai-ji organization. All major ceremonies and the ordinations of all oshos take place here. Although Mount Baldy Zen center is the main training center, Roshi still conducts several Dai-sesshins at Rinzai-ji each year and gives daily sanzen when he is in residence.

RINZAI-JI
SOHAN, SHIKA
2505 Cimarron Street
Los Angeles, CA 90018
323-732-2263
office@rinzaiji.org
www.rinzaiji.org

LEFT CELEBRATING THE 44TH ANNIVERSARY OF ROSHI'S COMING TO AMERICA

RIGHT SOHAN YOUNGELSON, RINZAI-JI SHIKA

LEFT, CENTER

MOUNT BALDY ZEN STAFF

OVERLEAF

MOUNT BALDY ZEN CENTER, EARLY 1970S

MOUNT BALDY ZEN CENTER

Mount Baldy Zen Center was founded in 1971 and, since then, it has served as the main training center for Rinzai-ji. Each winter and summer Roshi leads intensive practice periods (seichus) there. Majestic Mount San Antonio, nicknamed Mount Baldy, towers 4,000 feet above the zen center, which is located at over 6,000 feet. Deep snows in the winter and desert heat in the summer contribute to the stark beauty of the setting.

MOUNT BALDY ZEN CENTER
KYOZAN JOSHU ROSHI
GENTO, SHIKA
P.O. Box 429
7901 Mount Baldy Road
Mount Baldy, CA 91759
909-985-6410, 909-985-4870 *fax*
www.mbzc.org
office@mbzc.org

The 100th Year of Joshu Sasaki Roshi

Rinzai-ji Temples and Centers

JEMEZ BODHI MANDA ZEN CENTER

Jemez Bodhi Manda Zen Center hosts Roshi for two shorter training periods each year in the spring and fall. With its beautiful hot pools and steep canyon walls, Bodhi provides an ideal setting for zen practice. Founded in 1972, Bodhi arose when Roshi fulfilled his promise, "You find hot springs, I come." The center hosts retreats from other groups during the summer and maintains a warm relationship with the surrounding community year round. Bodhi also has lovely vegetable and flower gardens as well as a small orchard.

JEMEZ BODHI MANDA ZEN CENTER
JIUN HOSEN, OSHO
P.O. Box 8
Jemez Springs, NM 87025
505-829-3854
505-709-0053 *cell*
office@bmzc.org
hosen1013@yahoo.com
www.bmzc.org

LEFT

THREE BODHI VICE ABBOTS, FROM LEFT: GENRO, SEIJU, AND GENTEI

RIGHT

ROSHI AND MICHELE MARTIN, FOUNDER OF JEMEZ BODHI MANDA

The 100th Year of Joshu Sasaki Roshi

TOP

MAIN ALTAR OF SUTRA HALL AT BODHI MANDA
FROM LEFT: KOJUN, SHUNKO, ROSHI, HOSEN, TEISHIN AND SHOREN

BELOW

BODHI MANDA HOT POOLS
SUTRA HALL

Rinzai-ji Temples and Centers

ALBUQUERQUE ZEN CENTER
KOZEN JI
KOGAN SEIJU, OSHO
 2300 Garfield Avenue SE
 Albuquerque, NM 87106
 505-268-4877
 seiju@azc.org
 office@swcp.com
 www.azc.org

BLUE RIDGE ZEN GROUP
TEIDO BILL STEPHENS
 4425 Advance Mills Road
 Earlysville, VA 22936
 434-973-5435
 brzen@adelphia.net
 www.home.adelphia.net/~brzen

BODHIDHARMA ZENDO WIEN
SEIUN GENRO, OSHO
 Fleischmarkt 16-1010
 Wien, Austria
 011-43-1-513-3880
 bodhidharma@hotmail.com
 www.bodhidharmazendo.net

CENTRE ZEN DE LA MAIN ENPUKU-JI
ZENGETSU MYOKYO, OSHO
30 Rue Vallieres
Montreal, PQ H2W 1C2
Canada
514-842-3648
czmain@dsuper.net
www.centrezendelamain.ca

CENTRO ZEN DE PUERTO RICO CHO ON JI
GENTATSU, OSCAR PEREIRA
La Cumbre
497 Avenue Emiliano Pol
Apartado 186
San Juan, Puerto Rico 00926
787-720-5578, 787-397-2953 *cell*
www.centrozen.org
gentatsuopereira@yahoo.com

DENKYO-AN
HARUYO SASAKI
2249 West 25th Street
Los Angeles, CA 90018
323-737-5521

DESERT HOT SPRINGS
HARUYO SASAKI
12280 Miracle Hill Road
Desert Hot Springs, CA 92240
760-329-3912

LEFT

ALBUQUERQUE ZEN CENTER

CENTER

CENTRO ZEN DE PUERTO RICO

RIGHT

MRS. HARUYO SASAKI

Rinzai-ji Temples and Centers

LEFT

HAKU-UN-JI ZENDO

RIGHT

ITHACA ZEN CENTER

HAKU-UN-JI
HAKUUN SOKAI, OSHO
1448 East Cedar Street
Tempe, AZ 85281
480-894-6353
sokai@zenarizona.com
www.zenarizona.com

HOGAKU- JI HEKI UN ZAN
SEIDO, OSHO & SHUNKO
Grand Junction, CO 81504
970-434-3522
seidoclark@gmail.com

HOKOKU-AN ZEN CENTER
SEIDO RAY RONCI
805 Randy Lane
Columbia, MO 65201
573-875-5428
raymarly@earthlink.net
zen.Columbia.Missouri.org/
hokokuan

HOLLYWOOD ZEN CENTER
SEIGAKU KIGEN, OSHO
8261 Fountain Avenue, #6
West Hollywood, CA 90046
323-552-6026
Kigen01@aol.com
www.Hollywoodzen.org

HOUN AN
KYOON DOKURO, OSHO & SHUKO
75 Sparks Street
Cambridge, MA 02138-2215
617-491-8857
www.unsui.org, info@unsui.org
dokuro@bu.edu

ITHACA ZEN CENTER
YOSHIN, OSHO & KOGETSU
56 Lieb Road
Spencer, NY 14883
607-272-0694
info@bodymindretreats.com

JOSHU ZEN TEMPLE
GISAN KODO, OSHO &
HOON MYOSEN, OSHO
1401 Camino Real Circle
Hemet, CA 92543
951-766-9153
myosenmo@wmconnect.com

KAKUSHO-JI
ZUIUN GIKO, OSHO
    4206 Marquette Avenue NE
    Albuquerque, NM 87108
    505-328-2145
    giko@earthlink.net

LITTLE ZENDO OF ENTSU–JI
SHOZAN MARC JOSLYN, OSHO
    8842 Mandus Olsen Road
    Bainbridge Island, WA 98110
    206-842-2828
    entsujizen@zipcon.net

LONG ISLAND ZEN CENTER
GENSHIN, OSHO
    6 Brewster Street
    Setauket, NY 11733
    631-751-8408
    edkann@optonline.net
    www.zenli.org

MIAMI ZEN CENTER
SOUN DANNY PAOLUCCI
    2219 SW 59th Avenue
    Miami, FL 33155
    305-266-0830
    ahimandan@aol.com

MYOKO NI SORIN
JIKO MYOKUN, OSHO
    P.O. Box 1350
    Cobb, CA 95426
    707-928-4120
    myokun@jps.net
    www.myokonisorin.org

MOUNT COBB SAISHO ZEN-JI
Gido, Osho & Eko, Osho
    P.O. Box 1290
    Cobb, CA 95426
    707-928-5667
    gido@hughes.net
    eko@hughes.net

MOUNT GAZING ZEN CENTER
KOJUN & JUNDO
    1597 Road 30
    Dolores, CO 81323
    970-882-2530
    diron@fone.net

NORTH CAROLINA ZEN CENTER
KOZAN GENTEI, OSHO
    390 Ironwood Road
    Pittsboro, NC 27312-6754
    919-542-7411
    sandystewart@prodigy.net
    nczencenter@prodigy.net
    www.nzccenter.org

LEFT

PUGET SOUND ZEN CENTER

RIGHT

NORTH CAROLINA ZEN

CENTER

Rinzai-ji Temples and Centers

PRINCETON ZEN SOCIETY
CHINZAN FEHMI, OSHO
317 Mount Lucas Road
Princeton, NJ 08540
609-924-0782
lesfehmi@ix.netcom.com

PUGET SOUND ZEN CENTER
GAKUDO KOSHIN, OSHO
P.O. Box 2644
Vashon, WA 98070
206-463-4332
office@pszen.org
www.pszen.org

ROKUON-JI
UNGAN KIDO, OSHO
P.O. Box 900079
Palmdale, CA 93590
661-265-9232, 323-228-0851 *cell*
ungankido@yahoo.com

TOKO JI
KYONEN JIM GORDON
1812 Hardscrabble Road
Roxbury, NY 12474
607-326-4501
Morezazen28@yahoo.com
www.maitreyahouse.com

UNIVERSITY ZEN CENTER
DAI GYO JI
JOZAN KOYO, OSHO
115 South 42nd Street
Boulder, CO 80305
303-440-6553
zen@colorado.edu

UPPER VALLEY ZEN CENTER
GENDO ALLYN FIELD
58 Bridge Street
White River Junction, VT 05001
603-448-4877, 603-448-1411
Allyn.field@valley.net
www.UVZC.org

VICTORIA ZEN CENTER
ESHU KARL MARTIN
4970 Nagle Raod RR #6
Sooke, BC V0S 1N0
Canada
250-642-7936
eshu@zenwest.ca
www.zenwest.ca

WILLIAMSBURG ZEN CENTER
TOKUJU GENSHU, OSHO
119 North 11th Street
Brooklyn, NY 11211
646-591-9874
genshu@earthlink.net
wzc.rinzaiji.org

ZEN CENTRE OF VANCOUVER
HOJU ESHIN, OSHO
4269 Brant Street
Vancouver, BC V5N 5B5
Canada
604-879-0229
www.zen.ca
eshin@zen.ca

Williamsburg

TEKIO, OSHO
331 Breezes Road
Aranui, Christ Church 8007
New Zealand
011-64-3-960-5274

ZEN IN AUGSBURG
HOGEN HERIBERT HARTER
Neidhartstrabe 13
86159 Augsburg
Germany
001-8-21-55-0696
hogen@zen-augsburg.de
www.Zen-augsburg.de
www.Zenbuddhism.info

**BODHIDHARMA ZENDO
DÜSSELDORF**
SHINGEN GAENSSLEN
Bruchstrabe 13-15 40235
Düsseldorf 40629
Germany
0049/(0)211 / 22 95 016
shingen@shingen.de
www.zen-duesseldorf.de

DOAN, OSHO & SHOREN
1113 West 10th Street
Mesa, AZ 85201
480-668-0866
doan@fastq.com

Rinzai-ji Temples and Centers

PAGE 59

FROM LEFT: KYONEN JIM GORDON, LEN JOHN PINTO, GENSHU OSHO, DOAN OSHO, ROSHI, SHOREN, KOYO OSHO, AND GENSHIN OSHO. MYOSHIN RITA KANN, WHO PASSED AWAY FEBRUARY 11, 2007, IS SEATED IN THE CENTER.

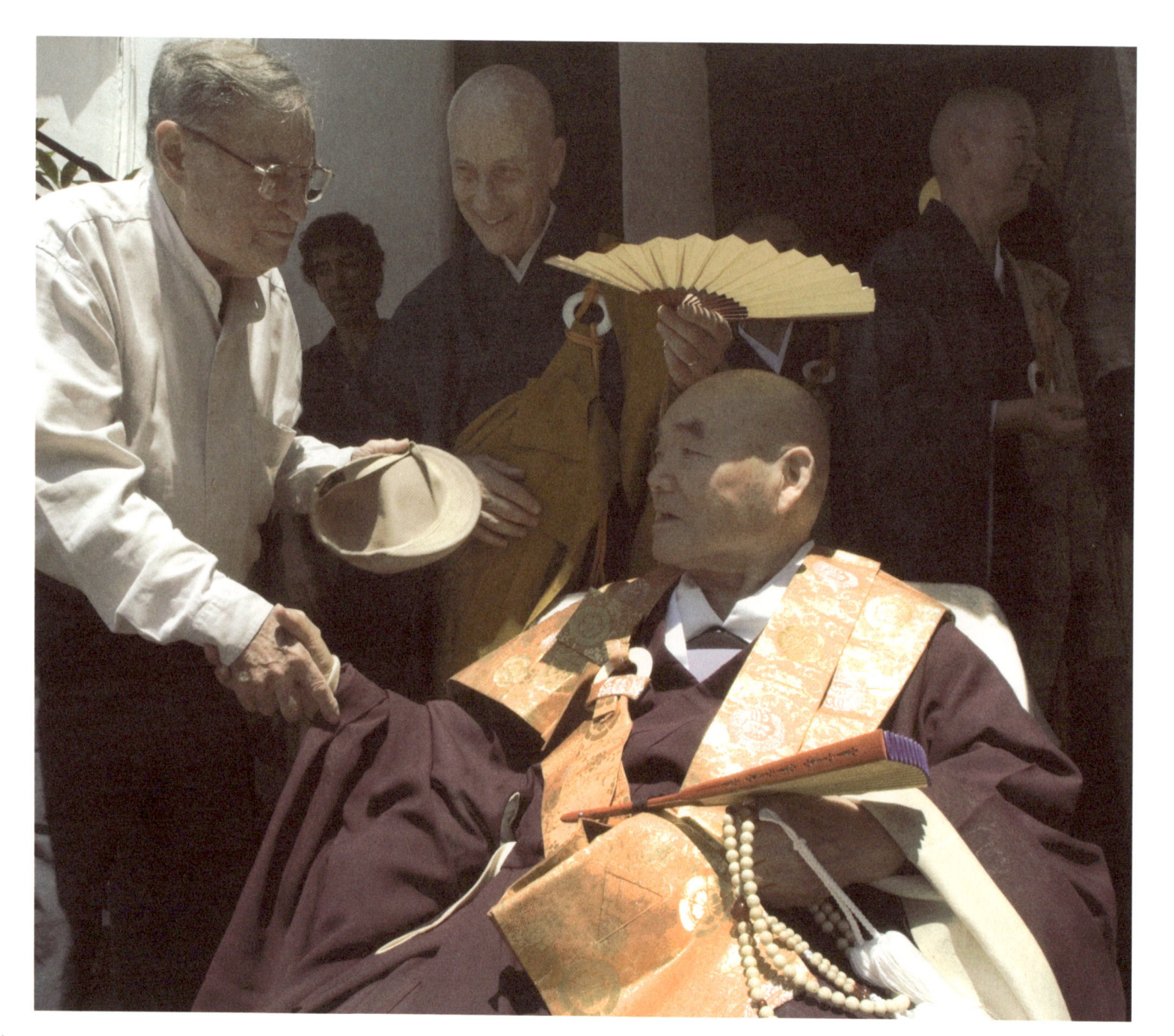

60
The 100th Year of Joshu Sasaki Roshi

SOME REFLECTIONS

GENTEI STEWART

My interest in Buddhism was first aroused when I was sixteen. I heard Alan Watts speak on a radio station in Berkeley, California. His Zen stories intrigued me and left me wondering if Zen was actually a religion.

My training with Joshu Roshi began when I was twenty-nine. I heard him interviewed on Radio Free Oz by his student, Peter Bergman. When I heard of Roshi's recounting how he had answered spontaneously to his master Joten Roshi's question, "How old is Buddha?" – "Buddha's age and my age are the same" – I immediately wanted to meet him. I drove straight to the radio station where Peter directed me to the Mariposa Rinzai Zen Dojo in Gardena.

Various incidents during my years of training with Joshu Roshi have made unforgettable impressions on me. Often, during teisho, or when Roshi is making deep bows at the altar, I am moved to tears by his immeasurable generosity, perseverance and patience with his students.

In 1973, I was ordained as an Osho and became vice-abbot of the Cimarron Zen Center (now Rinzai-ji) in Los Angeles. In

SHOZAN AND MYODO JOSLYN

1975, I was appointed abbot of the Jemez Bodhi Manda Zen Center in Jemez Springs, New Mexico. For the past thirty years, I have been very fortunate to serve as Abbot of the North Carolina Zen Center near Chapel Hill.

The roots of the North Carolina Zen Center were established in 1972 when Susanna Stewart formed a sitting group in her home north of Pittsboro. After attending several Dai-sesshins with Roshi, she decided to build a small zendo near her home so that Roshi would have a place to give sesshins on the East Coast. This became known as the Squirrel Mountain Zendo of the North Carolina Zen Center, which was incorporated in 1977. That same year, Susanna and I were married.

In 1995, knowing that for many years I had envisioned the creation of a residential Zen center, one of my students gifted fifteen acres of land near the North Carolina Zen Center. Shortly thereafter, construction of the Brooks Branch Zendo began. The mediation hall was completed in 1998, the kitchen in 2001, a multi-use/dormitory building was built in 2003 and the shower house was completed in 2005. A dormitory/dining hall and a larger meditation hall are now in the planning and fund-raising stages.

I consider the large number of wonderful students who continue to practice here and support the center to be a great good fortune.

SHOZAN JOSLYN

I heard about Roshi in 1962, when he first arrived in America. Religious phonies were known to thrive in California so I did not follow through until two years later when a friend chided me for my fear of being disappointed that the Roshi might not be genuine.

For a while after starting practice I would drive from Claremont (where I was living) to Gardena to sit with Roshi and others in his garage which had been fixed up as a zendo. I started a group in Claremont and persuaded Roshi to come there for sanzen on Monday evenings.

In Los Angeles, Roshi had attracted quite a following. And with that following enough money was raised to buy a place more central than Gardena and more suited to the needs of a growing sangha. In 1968, several of us were able to put up enough money to buy the Cimarron property in Los Angeles, formerly a Catholic school. From then on Roshi had a place to live as well as a place to conduct proper sesshins and other traditional Zen activities.

In 1970 I began an inquiry about property up the Mt. Baldy road. After several weekends of futile searching, I learned that the Boy Scouts of Pasadena wanted to sell their summer camp, a 99-year lease on Forest Service land high up on the 6500 ft. level of Mt. Baldy. The following weekend, I drove there to have a look. What I encountered was quite discouraging. There was a certain crude attractiveness to the site but looking inside the cabins was a shock. The cabins had been vandalized inside. Apart from broken windows and strewn trash like decayed food, discarded clothing, condoms, and feces were everywhere. Neverthe-less, through the hard work of many students, this became Mount Baldy Zen Center.

In 1972, along with several other fellows, I was ordained a monk at MBZC by Roshi. In 1974, my wife Hajni and I purchased a cabin on Mount Baldy, about a fifteen-minute drive from the center. The cabin burned down in 1979. It took two and a half years to rebuild.

In 1986 we moved to Bainbridge Island in Washington and found a place we could afford . . . 2.5 acres and a house. We sold our cabin on Mount Baldy and bought this place. We planted fruit trees, a vegetable and flower garden, got some chickens, and so forth. A little while later we opened The Little Zendo of Entsu-ji (according to Koshin, Roshi commented that Entsu-ji means "free of God, free of human") on the property.

SEIJU MAMMOSER

I became interested in Zen by accident while reading a book on Buddhist meditation and it awakened me to a hunger that had been hidden within me. After working my way through every Zen book I could find in the bookstores, I still wasn't satisfied. With my student loan payments finished, I had enough money for a used car and the need to find out, "What if . . ."

I found my way to Mt. Baldy soon after the conclusion of summer seichu in 1974. Roshi wasn't there – only the skeletal staff

Inka (transmission) is manifest when finally the student's thinking agrees with the teacher's thinking. When the teacher says, "Your kensho's thinking and my kensho's thinkng are absolutely the same as each other," that is when for the first time inka has been manifest. There is the Dharma activity of the teacher. When the teacher is astounded by your Dharma activity, then inka is manifest.

of monks; yet I was drawn to the opportunity. After arranging my affairs back in Chicago, I stayed at Mt. Baldy through the winter seichu, five months in all. At the end of seichu I was offered a scholarship to stay on, but I had had enough. Certainly Roshi was amazing, but the monks were remote and difficult to connect with, and the formal structure felt stifling. I returned to Chicago, trying to lose myself in my old life and old friends, but I couldn't. I knew I was avoiding something that felt deeply true only because it was terribly difficult. I had to return to Roshi and Mt. Baldy.

The next two years I returned to Mt. Baldy for seichu, but left immediately afterwards. Over time I made peace with the structure of formal practice and accepted another offer to stay on as a staff person. I wasn't interested in becoming a monk; I just wanted more practice with Roshi.

While I was training as tenzo, Roshi offered a series of classes in Los Angeles for his monks and nuns. Lay students were not allowed. I realized that if I wanted to deepen my practice I would need to make a further commitment. I still didn't care to be a monk, but I wanted more thorough training from Roshi. I wrote Roshi a letter to this effect and his reply was, "You must become monk," so, that was settled.

After living at Mt. Baldy for over three years, Roshi needed someone to manage Bodhi Manda after Gentei left. The monks senior to me didn't accept the offer. I wasn't looking to leave, but I said I would go if he needed me to. Roshi sent me to Bodhi in the Summer of 1980.

After nine years at Bodhi and many changes, I felt the need to do something different. Some of Roshi's students in Albuquerque wanted to start a Zen center and I saw this as an opportunity for a fresh beginning. I moved to Albuquerque in August of 1989 and Roshi dedicated the Albuquerque Zen Center on November 11, 1989.

The focus of the Albuquerque Zen Center has always been on offering daily practice for people with obligations to family and work. It is "commuter Zen" with a daily schedule designed to allow people to participate as much or as little as their schedule and commitment allow. Besides daily zazen there are weekly discussion classes, dharma talks, and monthly one-day sits for busy but interested Albuquerque students. For the first several years I was working an outside job along with everyone else. It was only in 1994 that I was able to devote myself full-time to the center and rely on the sangha's generosity.

Since 1989, the Center has grown to keep up with Albuquerque's burgeoning interest in Zen. After purchasing a piece of land below the University of New Mexico, we were able to raise the money to build the current center. In 1997, Roshi dedicated the new zendo, and we held a four-day sesshin to celebrate the occasion. The new facilities include a meeting room, library, and living quarters. In these quiet spaces, students can take time away from the noise and complexity of their everyday lives to participate in zazen, instruction group discussions and individual study.

As for myself, I am grateful to still be studying with Roshi and to encourage my students to participate in Dai-sesshins with him as well.

ESHIN GODFREY

When I was 14 years old, I became conscious of the transition taking place as I passed from childhood into adulthood. I sensed that something precious was being left behind, a brightness of consciousness. In my early thirties, I met the Tibetan Lama Yeshe and was convinced that he still possessed what I had lost. This started my interest in Buddhism.

At that time, Roshi was coming to New Zealand annually to give Dai-sesshin. After participating in my first sesshin, I intuitively felt that zazen was my natural way. It was very direct and it put me in touch with myself – something I had long been yearning for.

After three years of participating in the annual New Zealand Dai-sesshins, I decided to go to Mount Baldy Zen Center for training.

During teishos, Roshi gave detailed and helpful instructions on breathing. I paid close attention to these instructions and applied them seriously. They enabled me, over time, to steady my mind and integrate it with my breathing body. Later I found this centeredness and openness could be extended into every-

BELOW

HANAMATSURI,

RINZAI-JI ZEN CENTER

day life, allowing me to be more clear-minded while engaged in activity.

Joshu Roshi was first invited to Vancouver in 1967 in response to a general interest in Buddhism. A zazen group developed as a result of this visit and later called itself the Zen Centre of Vancouver.

I was invited to lead the group in 1985 and continued the daily zazen and monthly one-day sits. Longer retreats were started in 1990 with two- and three-day retreats every four to six months. Later, five-day sesshins were started, then seven-day sesshins, building up to four a year as demand grew. By 1995 zendo attendance had increased enough to move to a larger property. Late that year the present property on Brant Street was purchased. By 1999 the small zendo at Brant Street became inadequate and a renovation project was started to double its size and to provide an apartment for the resident monk. By 2001 the project was nearly complete, and members were doing the finishing work. It was a project that brought the sangha closer together and made it stronger. Now, in 2007, larger facilities are again required and a project team is researching options.

Sincere and deep gratitude must be given to the many committed, serious Zen students who have upheld the practice for over thirty years and to the current directors who all have mature life and business experience to contribute to the administration. No matter what happens I will do my best to continue Roshi's teaching and effort. We must all do this. In this way he will appear again in our teachings and efforts, and his great effort will not have been in vain.

MYOKUN SEGHESIO

I first met Joshu Roshi during spring break from the University of New Mexico. It was my first experience with formal practice. Until then, I had been on my own – sitting, dreaming and waiting. That spring, I spent two weeks at Bodhi Manda Zen Center and the following winter I did my first Rohatsu Daisesshin. I was hooked. Early on, I realized that this practice needed deep focus, complete release and real courage. I struggled with all three, and still do today.

In the winter of 1983–84 I was the first woman to be assigned the role of shoji during the seichu training period at Mt. Baldy Zen Center. In those days, only the shoji or sho-shoji cleaned the chemical toilets and dumped Roshi's toilet (which was kept in a closet near the sanzen room). There was a lot of snow that winter and by the end of those six months, my hands were so swollen from exposure to the chemicals and freezing weather that I almost lost a finger.

I was ordained a nun the following March.

I decided to help women serve in officer training positions and this remains my goal to this day. To date, very few women have served in the positions of jikijitsu and shoji. I am grateful to be in a position to pass along my training to women at Myoko Ni Sorin, our training and practice center in northern California.

Currently, I am working to establish a sister center to Myoko Ni Sorin, a new city center named Dharma Heart Zen Center. It is my goal to have these two centers work hand and hand. Given Roshi's advanced age, I feel it is important to maintain a living, breathing practice, to actively manifest all those years of training instead of just sitting on them. I hope that some day my efforts will begin to repay Roshi's kindness.

MYOKUN SEGHESIO

LEFT

YOSHIN AND ROSHI

CENTER

KOGETSU RADIN

YOSHIN RADIN

I was raised in a religious Jewish family and attended parochial schools through high school. It provided a great deal of discipline which was useful in Zen practice later on. The death of both my parents while I was still young made me wonder why people would seriously pursue goals and lives that would inevitably turn to dust.

During the sixties, in college and after, I experimented with hashish and LSD and had some experiences that pointed me to Buddhism. After seven years of hippie life and riding this roller coaster, I read *Buddha is the Center of Gravity*, a pamphlet of Roshi's teishos during a sesshin at the Lama Foundation. I thought, "Now here is someone who knows these things without tripping or smoking!"

I called Mount Baldy to find out his schedule. It was a few days before Rohatsu, 1976 which I decided to do. Genro was the shika and remarked, in his heaviest Austrian accent, "Are you sure you vant to do this? It's a rrreal ballbuster!"

A year later my first child was born and she was named Joshi – a gesture to Joshu. More children followed and so I went to sesshins without ever taking up long residence in a training center.

The dissolution of the hippie commune where I had lived for 10 years evolved into Beech Hill Pond Meditation Center and Roshi visited to give sesshin from 1978–1980. There was no electricity, running water or telephone. Chanting was by candle light. In teisho, Roshi frequently referred to Shakyamuni as "the king of the hippies."

When my wife and I divorced in 1980, it led to the end of Beech Hill Pond and the appearance of Ithaca Zen Center. It also provided a lesson about impermanence. In 1984 I married Kogetsu, my closest friend for thirteen years and, in 1986, we purchased 60 acres of land outside Ithaca which has been the home of IZC for the last twenty years. In 1991 the center burned to the ground. Roshi and several members of Rinzai-ji sent us support to help at that difficult moment. Since then the center has been re-built and serves as a retreat and Zen practice facility.

To have met a teacher who so clearly and intensely brings the Buddha's wisdom into this world has been a great blessing in my life.

JOSHI AND JOSHU

PEOPLE SAY, ROSHI, TAKE IT EASY, CUT DOWN ON YOUR SANZEN, YOU NEED TO REST. FROM A HUMAN PERSPECTIVE, YES, THAT'S A GOOD THING TO SAY. BUT MORE IMPORTANT IS TO MANIFEST ZERO, AND FOR THIS, PRACTICE IS NECESSARY.

I HAVE BEEN IN THIS COUNTRY OVER FORTY YEARS. AND THE MAIN PROBLEM PEOPLE HAVE IN THIS CULTURE IS THAT THEY ARE CONVINCED THAT SELF IS A THING, AN ENTITY.

SOKAI BARRATT

A strong emphasis on zazen and frequent sesshins first attracted me to practice with Roshi in 1975. I had never studied with any other dharma teacher before. My training began with winter Seichu in 1980 at Mt. Baldy Zen Center.

I fondly remember Roshi instructing me on the dharma activity with no translator present . . . just the two of us in his living room at Rinzai-ji. I thought how wonderful it was that such a great teacher would go to such lengths to teach a student.

Another time, during Seikan at Mt. Baldy, Roshi asked a group of monks and nuns whether there should be sanzen in the evening. There was a vote and all except one said Roshi was too tired and there should not be sanzen. That evening there was sanzen; I understood then that when Roshi is around one must be ready for sanzen at any time.

When I felt ready, I suggested to Roshi that I start a Zen center in Nevada. "Very good," he said, then after pausing for a moment, "Phoenix better." As soon as I arrived in Phoenix, I started advertising the zendo sitting schedule; nobody came. This went on for six months and I wanted to go home. Somehow I persisted, and slowly people started attending. Since 1994, I have been very happy as Abbot of Haku-un-ji Zen Center and the sangha has been very kind to Shinkai and myself.

With deep gratitude I will continue my sanzen training with Roshi as long as possible.

KIDO BERHOW

Two distinct experiences brought me to Zen Buddhism. The first occurred on September 25, 1978 at 9:01 AM when I witnessed the nation's third worst mid-air accident. The body of the pilot of a small plane plummeted to the ground one block from where I and hundreds of stunned on-lookers watched. The fatally crippled 727 seemed to float motionless for a few moments before rolling over and diving away. The indelible vow that I made that morning – watching a silent, black mushroom cloud – was that I would try to understand our world. I was fourteen.

My training with Joshu Roshi began the summer of 1987. Arriving at Mt. Baldy Zen Center on June 28, my intention was to complete summer seichu and write my final college thesis on my immersion in an authentic Zen environment. Late that summer, near the end of the training period, I formally asked Roshi if I could become a resident and monk at Mt. Baldy Zen Center.

After living at Mt. Baldy for nine years, I was sent to Mt. Cobb for a year and a half, whereupon I returned to Rinzai-ji. Roshi made it clear I wasn't to stay at Rinzai-ji. After one year at Rinzai-ji two students from Antelope Valley offered to partially donate a house and property if Rinzai-ji could make up the remainder. "Would I consider starting a center in Palmdale?" they asked.

Starting a new center was a great challenge. There was no car, the utilities were off, and only by the grace of a friend who came over that evening, was there food to eat. Our first butsudan was a box with a Buddha on top. Zafus were non-existent, so we used pillows, futons and chairs. We grew our food in the garden.

The sangha is on the upswing. We recently completed a road and sidewalk improvement. The construction of a temple is still years away. The zendo remains the living room but it is now adorned by a hand-made butsudan, tans and zabutans. Everything in the room has been donated or assembled by students.

KIDO BERHOW

KIGEN EKESON

An annoying mixture of curiosity and angst attracted me to Zen practice. I first studied Zen with Myo-on Maurine Stuart-Freedgood at the Cambridge Buddhist Association for two years before meeting Roshi. After meeting him, I moved into Gentei-an in October of 1988 when Tekio was Shika and my first sanzen with Roshi as well as my shokenko ceremony both took place that December.

I have countless wonderful memories of my time with Roshi. One of my favorites is the night Kido, Koshin, Genshu and I were invited to have dinner with him. As usual, the inji made way too much food and Roshi urged us to completely finish the meal that had been prepared with such care for our benefit. In the middle of our meal, we all noticed a tiny feather floating slowly down from the ceiling. Silence ensued as all eyes focused on the feather hovering between Koshin and myself. Koshin held out a finger and the feather landed on it perfectly. I was transfixed by the sight and sat frozen – gawking at it. Suddenly, Koshin blew the feather right into my staring face. Roshi laughed harder than I have ever seen him laugh.

Training with Roshi, there are "insight" insights and "lack of insight" insights. At various times, I have had bright epiphanies into the nature of Mind; but what far outnumber these positive insights are the thousands of times I've failed to see things clearly.

In the end, when I consider how to thank Roshi for all he has shown me, I wonder how I could ever say "thank you" to my arms or my legs or my brain or my body? He is always with me.

KOSHIN CAIN

I started practicing with Roshi in February 1990 when I was 24. I had traveled to Mt. Baldy for Dai-sesshin once before with Gentei, my first Zen teacher. I got nowhere with Roshi in sanzen and my body hurt terribly during the week, but I came home ready to sign up for seichu!

My first summer at Baldy, I was deadly serious. I lost weight, hardly talked, didn't open any mail from home and sat overtime every night. My koan that summer was, "Christ died, went to heaven, went to hell, and on the third day resurrected. How do you resurrect?" It frustrated me greatly – I didn't know how to die yet, so how was I supposed to know how to resurrect? In retrospect, I think Roshi was trying to call me forward, out of my death march and into real Zen practice which encompasses both death and life. Today as a teacher, I sometimes think to myself: "Don't forget about resurrection!"

As I continue to trip through this life of mine, I often think of my days at Mt. Baldy. Even more than that, I think of Roshi's style. When I'm stuck in an emotion, I remember the way he moved effortlessly from one emotion to another. When I'm unsure of how to act, I remember his love for the bold move. When I feel bad about the little double-wide trailer we live in, I think of Roshi's cramped quarters at Baldy. I remember once trying to fix his sanzen buzzer box and saying I'd be right back with the right tool. He insisted that I not go, that we can fix it with what we had on hand. We ended up using duct tape of course. That was Roshi style.

It seems to me that above all, Roshi refused to stop moving, changing, experimenting. When he was in his early 90s he told me, "I should live ten more years. I am still learning, much to learn. I know sake is bad for me. But I like sake. I drink sake. I should investigate. Still learning…"

I am thankful to him for many, many other things as well: for his willingness to make all kinds of trouble in order to make a point and for setting up a cold, hard practice and leading it with such a warm heart.

I am deeply thankful to Roshi for the great effort he pours into his life and the people in his life. I am thankful to have been the recipient of some of that effort, thankful for whatever part of that example has rubbed off on me, and thankful for the part that hasn't – that shames me into working harder every time I see him.

KIGEN AND GENSHU

GENSHU RO

From very early in my life, the act of pure seeing has been a way for me to experience something deeper than the thinking mind. In Zen practice, the notion of just sitting, purely experiencing reality as it is, with the guidance of a legitimate spiritual teacher to boot, was very appealing. My very first taste of Zen practice came from being served a hot cup of tea in a cold zendo on a dark night in the middle of nowhere. Then, after sleeping a few hours, without speaking or hearing a word, returning for a cup of hot tea, in a cold Zendo on a dark night in the middle of nowhere. This first impression just felt very profoundly correct to me; it was in 1988 at Bodhi Manda Zen Center.

Having Roshi as a spiritual teacher has been incomparable. It is a different kind of love than the love one has for one's lover, one's children, or one's parents. The scholastic side to his teaching has a clarity and depth which I never found anywhere else. Complementing this is the practice which he teaches – one moment with one's entire body completely engaged in whatever activity is at hand; the next moment returning to the thinking, human self realizing this whole world and everything in it is a reflection of oneself. This is what I try to practice in my life.

I came to New York City in 2002 to be with my wife-to-be Maureen Ellenhorn. Hearing the chanting and seeing the black robes, a neighbor asked what kind of satanic rituals we were doing in there. However every time that I have been invited to give a talk to people interested in Buddhism, they have always responded quite readily to what I was saying and this has been encouraging. I am happy whenever someone expresses a genuine interest in Zen, comes to practice, or offers some form of support.

GIDO SCHNABEL

I started practicing with Roshi in 1971. My first Dai-sesshin was at Lake Awosting in the Catskills. It was such a powerful experience; it was beyond anything else I had encountered. I determined that I would take up the way of Zen.

Over the next five years, I attended four seichu periods at Mt. Baldy. After that I lived and practiced full time at Rinzai-ji, sometimes with a "regular" job on the outside and sometimes without. I attended Dai-sesshin at Mt. Baldy and Rinzai-ji whenever I could, usually several times a year. I was ordained as a monk in 1996.

For the past eight years, I have lived full time as a monk and Kanju of Mt. Cobb Sai Sho Zen-ji in northern California, together with my wife Eko who was ordained an osho in 2001.

GIDO SCHNABEL

That same year I also was ordained as an Osho.

Previous to encountering Roshi, I had no other Buddhist or Zen teachers of any consequence. He has been the complete inspiration for my immersion in Zen. For this, it is difficult to adequately express my gratitude to Roshi in words. Hopefully my life itself is, and will become, an expression of that gratitude.

DOKURO AND SHUKO

DOKURO JAECKEL

I began practicing Zen with Genro Seiun in the early 1980's in Austria after seeing him on television. I knew instantly that I had to try this. After a few years of practice, I met Roshi during the yearly Dai-sesshin he gave in Austria. Right then I knew I had found my Dharma master. The following year I signed up for summer seichu at Mt. Baldy and practiced there regularly for many years. During all that time I kept running a zendo in the town of Innsbruck, perched high on the fifth floor of a building erected in the twelfth century, while the tourists five floors down were participating in the local Tyrolean customs of dancing in lederhosen and yodeling.

I was ordained in 1989 and continued to commute between the world of a professional musician in Austria and the world of a Zen monk in the United States. In 1994, I decided to move to the U.S. to live with Shuko, whom I had gotten to know at Mt. Baldy during many training periods. We were married in 1995 and moved to Boston where we have been living ever since while continuing our studies with Roshi.

In 2004, through fortunate circumstances, I made contact with the Cambridge Buddhist Association (CBA) and was asked to lead the Zen group there. Since then, our small temple, which Roshi named *Hôun-an*, Dharma Cloud Hermitage, has been organizing Zen activities for the CBA. Our activities and our aspiration to create an autonomous Rinzai-ji Zen Center in the Boston area continue to this day.

Zen training and Roshi's teachings have had an impact pervading my entire life. I am greatly indebted to Roshi and the Sangha and thankful for the teachings of Tathagata Zen. It is a privilege and good fortune to have had the opportunity to encounter a master and human being of Roshi's caliber and, furthermore, to study with him.

GENSHIN KANN

I read a *New York Times Book Review* of *Zen Buddhism,* a book by D.T. Suzuki, containing the phrase, "A transmission from Mind to Mind without the use of words or letters." It was this phrase that stuck in my mind and first got me interested in Zen. I was 23 or 24 at the time.

I first met Roshi in the spring of 1972 at age of 42 at a Daisesshin hosted by Les Fehmi, now Chinzan Osho. Roshi gave sanzen at the back of an industrial kitchen in the manager's office which had one glass wall open to the kitchen.

After I told him that I was a mathematician, he asked, "How much is one and one?"

"Two," I replied.

"Nooo! One and one equals Zero," Roshi exclaimed, pointing out a principle of dissolution that I would study the rest of my years with him.

Many years ago Roshi gave our Long Island Zen Center a calligraphy consisting of three *kanji* meaning: *don't, afraid, give* – "Don't be afraid to give up your self to help all sentient beings." This is the most important and precious practice I have been teaching to my students ever since.

SEIDO CLARK, LEFT, AND
DOAN SCHABARUM

SEIDO CLARK

I started Zen practice with Roshi in 1974. Before then, I had read some books by D.T. Suzuki, Alan Watts, Philip Kapleau's *Three Pillars of Zen,* and so on. Inspired by these and others, I began studying with such teachers as Seung Sahn and Jan Chozen Bays and attended several sesshins.

Later, while at the Snowmass Trappist Monastery in Colorado, the Abbot told me that Joshu Roshi was going to provide a sesshin for the brothers. I asked him if I could attend as well and, after consulting with the other monks, he agreed.

Although I was drawn to thinking about Zen by books, it was Roshi's presence that drew me to real practice. From the very first encounter I had with Joshu Roshi and onward, I have been exposed to direct experience of Zen teachings. I've ended up training for thirty years at Mt. Baldy, Bodhi Manda and a few other Rinzai-ji Zen Centers.

Even after all this time, I am still inspired by Roshi's teachings. This spring, Roshi said in teisho, "Tathagata Zen commands and demands of us, 'Try this for yourselves. Try to do the loving activity through your breathing, all of the time.'" This is precious to me and I try to follow this practice in my everyday life.

Roshi officially opened our Zen center, Heki-un-zan Hogaku-ji, in Grand Junction, Colorado, in October 2001 at the end of a three-day sesshin. We had been sitting together for many years before Roshi officially opened our center.

I believe any words I could write could never come close to expressing the true gratitude I feel for my teacher and his teachings. Perhaps a simple sign of gratitude will be to continue my training and practice as long as I live.

Some anecdotes

We were having a drink together a few years ago. Roshi poked my arm, raised his glass, and said: "Excuse me for not dying."

During my second Dai-sesshin, Roshi told me in sanzen, "Zen does not believe in god; you *are* god-nature." This shook me profoundly, acknowledging a truth deep within me. After this experience, zazen took on a new purpose for me. I wanted to strip away the innumerable layers of habits, conditioning, confusion, falseness, and other stuff that made it difficult to see this clearly. This process took many, many years and was often punctuated with times of great inner turmoil.

During training, zazen was a struggle for me and I often fell asleep or unconscious with the effort. This also happened during teisho. In the middle of one teisho, I woke up just long enough to hear the words "you have to go through what you have to go through" before fading back into unconsciousness. These words led me to have a deep faith in the process of zazen. They also gave me faith when working through difficult situations in my everyday life. I ceased trying to fix myself and, in general, stopped being as goal orientated.

As my training progressed, I developed a greater understanding of Roshi's teachings and was able to relate them to my personal experience as well as to sanzen encounters. I developed a deep appreciation of Buddhism as a guide to living everyday life rather than as a theory or philosophy.

During a sesshin at Cimarron, I had to go to the kitchen on some errand. I was the shoji on that occasion. The tenzo was somewhere else but there was Roshi in his white kimono, seated on a stool, wearing his big glasses, intently reading something. I thought "Aha, this is a good time to put a Zen question to Roshi." So I walked over to Roshi and began to ask, but Roshi anticipated and answered before I could finish my sentence. "Not now" he said, "Here is only old Japanese gentleman reading newspaper."

RIGHT

GENTO, MOUNT BALDY SHIKA

One day, as I was sitting in the Mt. Baldy zendo, I experienced a strong, spontaneous urge to open my hand on the out-breath, and close it on the in-breath. As I did this, I felt my consciousness simultaneously expanding and contracting. At the next sanzen, before I had a chance to even say one word, Roshi looked at me, opened and closed his hand just as I'd been doing in the zendo, and announced, "Now you can give Zen talks," and rang his bell.

Another memorable time, while I was driving, Roshi sat next to me in the passenger seat sound asleep, mouth open, snoring. Sitting straight, trying to do zazen as I drove, I finally had an intense moment of very awake, energetic one-pointedness. Exactly at that moment, Roshi suddenly sat up and said, "You and I, one heart!" and then he went right back to sleep.

An insight into the foundation of Joshu Roshi's teaching came a year or so later while at Rinzai-ji during sanzen. Joshu Roshi had been prodding me to answer a certain koan. "Without this experience you cannot understand our tradition," he said. "You must answer, or cannot go forward. This must be completely clear." The answer had been coalescing for some time.

During sanzen that morning, I recited my koan to Roshi. Smiling and animated, he made a subtle gesture to evoke the desired experience. Erupting in my mind was both the answer, the manifestation of the answer and the profound implications it contained. Dumfounded, staring at the brown bowing mat, I gave a manifestation. Roshi laughed uproariously, ringing his bell in wide strokes. I failed to bow to him on my way out that morning, stumbling past the shika, also without a bow. Later, back in the zendo, I realized that my entire education prior to Zen practice had been worthless.

When summer turned to fall, Roshi started me on takahatsu, the practice of begging. Participating only one time with the out-going monk, I was left to find my way through the maze of mongers who distribute food near downtown Los Angeles. Though my chest was tight the first few times, this came to be what I still consider the best practice I was ever exposed to during my training. Roshi had brought this tradition with him, established it for his students to follow, and then allowed me to practice takahatsu for the next three and a half years. For anyone who has practiced takahatsu, it is painfully clear when you are manifesting the right view and when you fail. There was no better taskmaster and teacher. It is that formative practice, initially so challenging, that has helped me to practice in everyday life.

One day when I was Shika at Mt. Baldy, as is the custom, I went to Roshi's cabin 10 minutes before sanzen with some sort of business question that seemed quite important to me at the time. Roshi was eating a grapefruit. He ate that grapefruit so completely, so ferociously, carefully placing the skin together to form a cup on the table that I was dumbstruck and forgot all about what I wanted to ask him.

◆

During a sitting period, I attached to the idea that the only correct way to answer the koan was to stride straight over to Roshi in sanzen and knock him over. For the remainder of the period and throughout kinhin, I held tight to the plan and breathed and seethed so as to be intense enough to actually do it. I raced off to sanzen and was the second one there, so I had a few moments at the kancho bell to rivet my determination. But just as I was about to ring myself into sanzen, the thought occurred that maybe there is something wrong with this, maybe the fact that Roshi gave sanzen four times a day, everyday, his whole life, might mean that I am missing something. I suddenly became almost paralyzed with fear, and could only stagger into the room, and while bowing, with my mouth in the mat, let loose a blood curdling scream of chaos and panic. Roshi immediately said, "Even there I love you. Anywhere you go, I love you." Then he rang the bell.

◆

One winter when I was Shoji, I came down with a bad flu a couple of days before Christmas. On Christmas Eve I still had a high fever and on Christmas morning, just as dawn was breaking, there was a loud rap on my door. The door swung open and Roshi stepped in, staff in hand, looking like an elf in a purple hooded cape someone had made for him. "You OK?" he asked.

"OK, Roshi," I said. He came over and felt my forehead, stood there for a moment, and said "Roshi worried." Then he turned and left, all the way back up those treacherous steps that this 90-year-old had somehow negotiated his way down in the wind and cold. I hope that I have exactly that spirit at 50, 60, 70, even at 100. I am grateful now, and I'm sure I will be for my whole life, for his teaching and for his great big example that the self is unfixed.

My first meeting with Roshi, in December of 1966, was a memorable one. I arrived at the dentist's office in Gardena, California, which was serving as a Zen center for Roshi's few students at that time. I was racked with arthritic pain in all my limbs, especially in my knees. Just sitting on a cushion was enough to drive me out of my mind, but I had been so inspired by D.T. Suzuki's book, *Buddhism*, that I was determined to endure whatever was required. I wrenched my legs into a sitting position and immediately began to sweat in reaction to the pain.

When it came time for me to visit Roshi in sanzen, I omitted the customary bows and simply walked in and sat Indian-style in front of him. He really looked at me and I looked at him. I felt completely exposed. He commenced by saying some words I couldn't make out. He repeated those words and again I couldn't understand what he was saying. Again he repeated the same words and all I could do was shrug my shoulders and feel disappointed. Again he repeated the words and again I couldn't make out a single one.

Finally, he started with the first word of the sentence and said it over and over again with varying pronunciations until I understood it. He repeated this process with each of the remaining words until I understood them all. He never showed even an inkling of impatience throughout the interchange.

It seems to me Roshi knows the full range of human experience and isn't afraid of any of it. So many times when shika at Mt. Baldy, I would come to him with a question about what to do, and he would say, "Anything OK," or "Your idea OK." Or the few times I would cook for him and his well-being was in my young hands – "Anything OK." Now the truth is, anything was not OK, but I had the feeling that Roshi didn't mind watching things fall apart – he was flexible enough to take whatever came of it, and he knew that disaster was a great teaching tool. At least I had that feeling, after a number of disasters.

As a butterfly lost in flowers,
As a child fondling mother's breast,
As a bird settled on the tree,
Sixty-seven years of this world
I have played with God.

Joshu Roshi, 1974

ROSHI AND JIKAN LEONARD COHEN WITH PROFESSOR GADJIN NAGAO, RIGHT, AT THE AWARD CEREMONY.

IN PRAISE OF JOSHU ROSHI'S GREAT WORK

Joshu Sasaki Roshi's Zen and his efforts to transmit this Zen are unique in depth, in color and in grandeur. On the occasion of his receiving this award, I would like to sincerely offer my deepest congratulations.

Roshi, at the age of fifty five, rather than resting on his laurels and settling into a comfortable position, did just the opposite. He resolved to travel overseas and throw himself into an entirely new sphere of teaching. Just thinking of only this moves me to bow my head.

From the start talented young Americans gathered around Roshi, and as their numbers gradually increased, through a natural process of cooperation and discussion, the Rinzai temple of Cimarron in Los Angeles was created during Roshi's sixth year in America. Towering above the city to the northeast, Roshi founded a special training center in the forest on Mount Baldy, and furthermore, he made another similar training hall in Jemez, New Mexico, deep in the mountains, thus creating these three centers as the basis for his activity.

Among those who have received Roshi's teaching there is no small number who have received Dharma names, shaven their heads and become Zen monks or nuns and put on the black robes. Among these there are some who have returned to their home towns and opened their own temples under the umbrella of Roshi's Zen. You can find these temples in the United States, Canada and throughout Europe. You can see that Roshi has not been just sitting at Cimarron teaching his students, but rather, he has energetically traveled to these other centers, led sesshins, and spread his Zen throughout the world.

Roshi has also visited Christian monasteries and conducted sesshins there. It is unlikely anyone else but Roshi could have accomplished the feat of conducting sesshins even within a different religious context.

I first met him in the summer of 1978. At that time, there was a two month training period in progress and I was invited to lecture on general Buddhist topics. Every morning there was sanzen, and a teisho was given which was spiced with a colorful, earthy flavor – another signature of Joshu Roshi's Zen which you probably could not find anywhere else.

My deepest wishes for his good health to continue and increase his most honorable work.

Excerpts from a talk by the distinguished Professor Gadjin Nagao at a ceremony in Japan in 1996 at which Joshu Roshi was awarded the Buddhist Missionary Meritorious Award by the Bukkyo Dendo Kyokai (Organization for the Dissemination of Buddhism).

EXCERPTS FROM ROSHI'S Award Acceptance Speech

IN JAPAN 1996, TO RECEIVE THE BUDDHIST MISSIONARY MERITORIOUS AWARD

BACK PROFESSOR GADJIN NAGAO, ROSHI, MRS. NAGAO

FRONT JIKAN COHEN, KIDO OSHO, OSCAR MORENO

The reason I went to America was the kancho (head abbot) of Myoshin-ji ordered me to. He just said, "Hey you! Get over there!" I was to construct a branch temple of Myoshin-ji in America.

When you talk about disseminating Buddhism or transmitting Buddhism, what this means is actually living Buddhism – living a life which is itself Buddhism. So what I have been practicing since I went over to America is to live Buddhism. I have not done anything other than that.

All things have a home. When we are born, we are born along with our home. There are no existent beings without a home. Even though I crossed the ocean to America, I didn't lose my home. If you penetrate clearly into the tenet of "never losing your home," you will be able to manifest the wisdom that understands what "living Buddhism" is. My teaching, my "propagation of Buddhism" has simply been the practice of manifesting the wisdom of living Buddhism. Nothing else. There are no rewards or acknowledgments of services rendered for this kind of teaching.

The 100th Year of Joshu Sasaki Roshi

THE RINZAI-JI BOARD OF DIRECTORS IS GRATEFUL TO THOSE WHO MADE THIS ALBUM POSSIBLE. WE TAKE THE CREATION OF THIS COMMEMORATIVE BOOK AS AN OPPORTUNITY TO THANK OUR TEACHER, KYOZAN JOSHU SASAKI ROSHI, FOR HIS FORTY-FIVE YEARS OF WONDERFUL TEACHING IN AMERICA AND HIS DEDICATION TO US, HIS STUDENTS OF THE RINZAI-JI SANGHA. WE HOPE TO CONTINUE WITH HIM LEADING IN THE FUTURE AS HE CELEBRATES HIS 100TH YEAR OF LIFE.

JEFF CREEK

PRESIDENT, BOARD OF DIRECTORS

RINZAI-JI

We must make a history that is entirely standing up upon no-self. We must make ceremonies that are thoroughly, in every aspect, no-self. We must transmit a teaching that is thoroughly, down to every tiny corner, teaching the love of no-self. There is nothing true about Buddhism except for the manifestation of no-self.